SCOTLAND'S PAST IN ACTION

C
toC
n

Colin MacLean

N·M·S

NATIONAL MUSEUMS OF SCOTLAND

Published by the National Museums of Scotland
Chambers Street, Edinburgh EH1 1JF

ISBN 0 948636 88 2

© Colin MacLean and the Trustees of the National
Museums of Scotland 1997

British Library Cataloguing in Publication Data
A catalogue record for this book is available from the
British Library

Series editor Iseabail Macleod
Designed and produced by the Publications Office of
the National Museums of Scotland

Printed on Fineblade 115 gsm. Pulp from managed sustainable forests,
bleaching process elemental chlorine free
Printed in Great Britain by BPC Wheatons Ltd, Exeter

Acknowledgements

The author is grateful to all those who helped him in many ways, including
Herrick Bunney, Iseabail Macleod, David and Anne Maxwell, and Donald
Herrick Bunney, Iseabail Macleod, David and Anne Maxwell, and Donald
J Withrington. Thanks are due to John Kerr for information about Blair
Atholl Church, and also to Charles Allan/Longmans (*Farmer's Boy*), and
Tuckwell Press (*Your Father and I*).

Illustrations: Front cover, 4, 7, 8, 9, 11, 12, 13, 16 top, 17, 20, 25, 29, 30, 32, 39, 41,
ii bottom, iii bottom, 46, 48, 49, 51, 52, 57, 58, 62, 65, 68, 69: National Museums
of Scotland. Back cover: St Giles' Cathedral. 6: Crown Copyright, reproduced by
permission of Historic Scotland. 11: John Watson. 16 bottom, 21, 22, iv top:
National Gallery of Scotland. 18 top: Anne Maxwell. 18 bottom: Allan Maclean.
36, i: MS. 211, IV and MS.42. fol.72V, Edinburgh University Library. iii top: Trustees
of the National Library of Scotland. iv bottom: City Art Centre, Edinburgh. 61:
By courtesy of The Mitchell Library, Glasgow City Libraries. 73, 79: St Andrew
Press. 77: John Macleod

All illustrations credited SLA are from the Scottish Life Archive at the National
Museums of Scotland.

Front cover: *John Campbell preaching in St Giles*, titled '*A
sleepy congregation*', John Kay, 1785.

Back cover: *Angel piper, carving in the Thistle Chapel, St
Giles' Cathedral, Edinburgh.*

CONTENTS

GOING TO CHURCH

1 Worshipful company

Nothing is known of the thoughts or beliefs of the first people who came, around 6000 BC, to what is now called Scotland. In studying the tools, ornaments and pottery, or the dwellings and the graves that remain from the Stone, Bronze or Iron Ages in the centuries that followed, we may identify particular customs or developing cultures, but only a little can be concluded about what may be called faith or religion - or even superstition.

The revolving seasons, the forces of the now fearsome, now welcome elements, the impact of the landscapes, the fruit of the land, the fish from the sea, the birds of the air, these must all have contributed to some sense of wonder, also presumably to patterns of expectation - and to a will to survive. Animals could be enemies, friends or food. Other humans could be friends or foes, masters or servants. Conflict and hierarchy were inevitable within families, within and between groups large and small. At some stage humility and wonder must have led to concepts of the spiritual and the supernatural, also to the recognition of dominance by some humans over others. A kind of logic may then have led to attributes of submission, reverence and propitiation, manifested in practices of worship and in conforming to ritual.

Worship has been described as the first form of theatre, and an element of worship may be detected or assumed in many forms of art. Stone circles, like those in Lewis and Orkney, are thought by some to be religious sites. Some early burial sites provide evidence of ritual, indicating a formalization of belief within a community.

Going to church at Wanlockhead in the mid-nineteenth century - to an open air service rather than a building, after the break away from the Church of Scotland.

Stone circle at Callanish, Isle of Lewis.

Over the centuries, communities have assembled to observe rituals, religious and otherwise. By the eighteenth and nineteenth centuries, in many parts of Scotland communities gathered for what some called Holy Fairs. Holy Communion was the focus of a great sometimes unholy - social occasion like the Gairloch Communion in the early nineteenth century described in *A Hundred Years in the Highlands* by Osgood Mackenzie:

Owing to want of roads, wheel or steam, the Gairloch Communion used to be held only once in three years. Consequently it became a very great holy fair...People came from the neighbouring parishes, some 50 or 60 miles distant. This was considered a pleasant walk, not by the communicants merely, but by crowds who came, not to communicate, but to see the people and to hear the many clergymen. In Gairloch every hole or corner with a roof over it was got ready by strewing it with straw for the visitors' beds during the six nights of their stay.

Undressing during that time was never dreamt of by the crowd and washing was impossible! Our barns and stables were all scrubbed out and ready for visitors, and for days before the feast there was much killing and cooking of cattle, sheep and salmon, for all the hungry visitors who were expected...For Communion the people assembled close to the parish church in a field able to hold 3,000 people. In the bottom of the deep oval hollow at one end was the clergyman's preaching box, giving him shelter from the sun and rain. Wind could not blow there, and even a weak voice would float over the hollow clearly. In front of the pulpit the Communion tables extended to the farther end.

Linlithgow, with the palace and St Michael's Church.
John Slezer, Theatrum Scotiae, *about 1690.*

In Scotland, at the end of the twentieth century, going to church is still an act of community: and it is very much more. Whether to join in Holy Communion or in other forms of Christian worship, every Sunday more than half a million people in Scotland go to over 4,000 churches. Some congregations are small and independent; some belong to national or international churches which trace their history as institutions back to the origins of Christianity itself.

2 Church of Rome

A Roman province was established in Britain in the first century AD. By the second century some Christians were, it is assumed, among the civilian incomers. Third-century gravestones in Galloway have Christian markings on them. By the fourth or fifth century Ninian, an English bishop trained in Rome, is believed to have built a stone church at Whithorn and to have been the

Enamelled and gilt copper crozier from the twelfth century, found at Whithorn Priory, Wigtownshire. Croziers were pastoral staffs linked with Scotland's early saints and bishops.

earliest Christian missionary in Scotland. In the sixth century Columba, a monk and member of an Irish royal family, founded a monastery on Iona, created an organized Christian community and introduced Christianity to the Picts.

Legends tell of the many other saints who, in the centuries that followed, were identified with the spread of Christianity in Scotland. The saints' names have been perpetuated in buildings, place names and streets - from Abb and Andrew, Cuthbert, Fergus, Fittick and Kentigern to Machar, Magnus and Ternan - and also in some local festivals. The *Aberdeen Breviary* of Bishop Elphinstone (1510) lists 70 Scottish saints.

Following the dissolution of the Roman Empire, Christianity survived, mostly uncoordinated, in some abbeys and monasteries, and was observed or recognized or imposed by some rulers and kings. The twelfth century was to bring new order: a parochial system, providing Scotland's oldest surviving local institutions, was established. By 1200 most of the 1,100 medieval Scottish parishes were in being. Theoretically, every person in Scotland had a parish and priest. By the late Middle Ages, it is asserted, every Scot was - technically speaking - a Christian and a member

Detail from panels carved in the 1530s for Cardinal David Beaton. It shows the tree of Jesse.

of the international and unified Church of Rome. This Church in Scotland operated now in alliance with, now in conflict with, the monarch or with parliament.

The Roman Church of medieval times was not concerned with size of congregation nor was it engaged in competitive evangelism. In a parish church, daily offices were sung by vicars and chaplains, services not necessarily attended by the public. In the mornings Mass might be celebrated at several altars in separate chapels within the one building. Perhaps a chaplain, endowed by a wealthy family, was saying Mass for the family, its relatives and also for deceased relatives, for whom Purgatory might thereby be rendered tolerable. Some of those present were poorer folk hoping for a distribution of alms. Others merely sought shelter, the local church being the only open building or social centre available. The church, too, was a conveniently protected place for trade, sometimes the focus of a local fair.

3 Reformed and divided

There were many reasons for the Scottish Reformation of 1560. Some were internal to Scotland, such as political and personal corruption. Some were more general or external, associated with interpretation of the Bible and with the principle of access to vernacular translations of it. A new parish-based structure was introduced. Ministers were chosen by congregations, from which elders were drawn who worked with ministers in kirk sessions: these had wide oversight of the community. By the 1580s there was in place an organization of kirk sessions, presbyteries in groups of parishes, regional synods and national General Assembly, each a gathering of clerics and elders. In the seventeenth century there was recurring conflict between church and monarchy about which had prime authority in determining the style of church government and of worship. The conflict became intense with the attempted imposition of a Book of Canons in 1636 and of a Prayer Book in 1637. In protest, the National

Fathers of the Secession. This engraving shows (left to right) Thomas Muir, Ebenezer and Ralph Erskine, Alexander Moncrieff, James Fisher and William Wilson, leaders of the Secession which originated in 1733, the first major secession from the national Church of Scotland. SLA

Covenant (1638) was drawn up, asserting the church's right to freedom from state or crown control: it was signed in Edinburgh and gained wide support. Conflict persisted through Cromwell's reign. The reimposition of episcopacy in 1660 was paralleled by a strident Covenanting movement which rejected control by king or bishops. With the Revolution Settlement of 1689-90 presbyterianism was established as the acceptable state-supported form of church government. Episcopalians and Cameronians (named after a leading Covenanter) remained outside the national church.

By 1800 there were at least eight distinct denominations in Scotland, some resulting from schisms in the Church of Scotland. Some groups of presbyterians had seceded from the Church of Scotland because of the restoration by Queen Anne in 1712 of rights of patronage whereby, for instance, a local landowner, not the congregation, could select a minister for a parish. The issue of patronage was central to the decision of a large number of ministers and elders to leave the Church of Scotland in the 1843 Disruption to form the Free Church of Scotland. In the middle of the nineteenth century 3,395 recorded places of worship were provided by 40 denominations. Religious adherence is said to have grown from mid- to end-century, possibly even doubling, this alongside rapid urban growth with greater industrialization. Between 1831 and 1911 Scotland's population rose from 2.3 to 4.8 million. (It rose to 5.2 million by 1971 and by 1993 was 5.1 million). The United Free Church and the Church of Scotland united in 1929, thus bringing together most of those who had been in the three major Presbyterian groupings of the late nineteenth century (Church of Scotland, Free Church and United Presbyerian). In 1931 the newly united church, the established church in Scotland, had a total roll of 1.28 million.

Roman Catholicism had no appreciable presence in the century and a half after the Reformation. Interest in and support

Silver brooch commemorating the Disruption of 1843. It bears the dates of significant events in Scottish church history, the names of church leaders, and the Burning Bush (Exodus 3.2). The Burning Bush was adopted as a crest by several presbyterian churches: the Church of Scotland has used it since the seventeenth century.

Open-air service, a common event after the Disruption left many congregations without a church in which to worship.

for it survived in places: there was one sizeable pocket in the north-east, also groups in the south-west and the West Highlands and Islands (thanks in part to the activities of priests from Ireland). Identification with the Jacobites was unhelpful to the Roman Catholic Church in the eighteenth century. Throughout the nineteenth, immigration to the Glasgow area from Ireland increased rapidly, bringing a large number of Catholics. Also, later in the century Italian Catholics came to Scotland. By 1900, Catholic percentage attendances were said to be the highest in Scotland, this when Catholics constituted about ten per cent of the population of Scotland (by 1960 15 per cent). The concentration of Irish Catholics in and near Glasgow resulted in a distinct community, predominantly working-class, but with strong enough leadership to secure, by an Act of 1918, for itself and for many other

Catholics in Scotland, the provision of state-supported Catholic schools. These reinforced the separate denomination, sustained Catholic church attendance, and within a few decades raised the social status of Catholics in Scotland.

Scottish Episcopalianism had had recurring strength during the political fluctuations of the seventeenth century but in the eighteenth it suffered persecution. In 1792 an Act repealed penal statutes against Scottish Episcopalians, whose forms of worship were not then much different from those of most presbyterians. Episcopalian membership grew, and increased markedly from the late nineteenth century onwards, by 1930 reaching 134,000.

In the mid-1930s the *Scottish Churches Handbook* listed more than 40 religious denominations, ranging from the main Presbyterian, Episcopalian and Roman Catholic churches to the Salvation Army, Unitarians, Quakers, Glasites and five categories of Brethren. This list included Judaism, its Scottish community having its centre in Glasgow but being 'represented also in the other three cities and, to a lesser extent, in some of the larger towns'. From the eighteenth century onwards many Jews were able to graduate in Scotland, where the absence of religious tests allowed for a wider entry to universities than in England. The 1930s handbook also lists missions to the Jews, while pointing out that orthodox Judaism 'is, speaking generally, not a missionary faith'. Such a handbook 60 years later would, of necessity, have included the several religions of the new communities from the East.

A Scottish Church Census of 1994 (*Prospects for Scotland 2000*, ed Brierley and Macdonald 1995) confined itself to Christian churches. It found there were churches representing 50 different Christian denominations in Scotland, some of them having a single congregation. According to this Census, on one Sunday in October 1994 there were 575,000 adults in church in Scotland, 14 per cent of the adult population: 171,000 children under 15 years were in church or at Sunday School. Of the adults, 38 per cent (218,500) were members of the Church of Scotland which in that year had a total membership of 715,571. Attendance, adults and children, in other presbyterian churches is listed as 23,310, and in Episcopalian churches as 20,350. The Mass attendance of the Roman Catholic Church in 1994 was just under 250,000.

4 A story in stone

Over the centuries, religious groupings in Scotland have worshipped in various settings, outdoor and indoor, in buildings large and small, some proudly ornate, some proudly bare of decoration. Scottish church buildings and remains provide evidence today, as do countless artefacts and works of art, of great craftmanship and artistic achievement over the past 2,000 years, a record which was not broken (as has been claimed) by the Reformation, but rather diversified. While the Reformation brought condemnation of what was thought to be idolatrous art, much art of the period continued to be lively and colourful.

Even in comparatively well-educated Scotland, until the nineteenth century there was not mass literacy. Paintings, murals, sculpture, tapestries, woodcuts, wood panels and carvings, stained-glass windows, and even jewellery provided for medieval times what has been called the Bible of the Poor. Alas, only the privileged could have access to some of the most richly illustrated and costly manuscripts and books. Ordinary people saw the Bible story and miracles portrayed in works of art and sometimes in dramatic form.

In the Middle Ages, in rural and urban areas alike, church buildings dominated the horizons of inhabited Scotland. They continued to do so, their turrets and occasional crowns becoming impressive features in the landscape, until industrial and municipal buildings, factory chimneys, tower blocks, electricity pylons and broadcasting aerials competed for height if not for beauty. From the late eighteenth century onwards, high church steeples reached distinctively for the heavens: in nineteenth-century Scotland, denominational competition contributed appreciably

to the number of churches in both town and country.

In the seventeenth and again in the nineteenth century, oppression of one kind and another drove people to hold religious services in the open air or in improvised structures. Sometimes, from the seventeenth to the early twentieth century, the assembly (as at Gairloch, p6) was too large for the local

Preaching tents afforded preachers elevation and also some protection from the elements. They were used especially for open-air communion services when the congregation was too large for the local church.

Tent Preaching at Bothwell, *an unfavourable view of open-air services by James Howe (1780-1836). The 'tent' here is a portable pulpit.*

church: on these exposed occasions a simple portable pulpit, often called a tent, was erected for the preacher. During the first Assembly of the Free Church of Scotland in 1843, a London manufacturing firm occupied a nearby field in Edinburgh, pitched a large specimen tent (of the more conventional kind) and proceeded to take orders. Such tents, which became known as clootie kirks, offered some protection against the elements: they were later to be used by evangelical mission groups moving around Scotland in the summer months.

Most Scottish church buildings, however, have been remarkably durable. Some medieval churches were to be destroyed by military activity or by mob violence, some were deserted and fell into ruin. Some, even as ruins, such as Elgin Cathedral and the Border abbeys, are noble edifices. Today the Church of Scotland

Kelso Abbey. One of the great Border abbeys but a ruin when depicted by John Slezer in his Theatrum Scotiae *about 1690.*

Parish church, Iona, built in 1830 by Thomas Telford who was engaged by the government to design and build 32 churches and 43 manses in remote Highland and Island parishes. Anne Maxwell

Plan and elevation for a manse of two storeys, designed by Thomas Telford.

has 60 substantially medieval churches still in use, a few of them visited more by tourists than by worshippers.

In the Middle Ages, churches and cathedrals dominated the burghs then being built. The Hie Gait (High Street) and the Hie Kirk (parish church), perhaps alongside the local castle, were central to the life of a community, nobles and important burgesses living nearby, with tradesmen and other citizens distributed appropri-

Ground Floor.

Elevation.

ately. The monasteries were the main seats of learning until the fifteenth century when the three universities of St Andrews, Glasgow and Old Aberdeen were created as religious foundations. The medieval Church in Scotland established kirks, hospitals and schools in burghs: the earliest of the burghs had been introduced by King David I (about 1085-1153). The provision, distribution and maintenance of churches were patchy until the eighteenth century, especially in the Highlands where the national church was insecurely established.

With the industrial revolution, many churches were built to cater for the expanding urban population. Some town councils provided funding. Or a mill owner (as in Stanley, Perthshire, in the 1820s) might build a company church, as well as a company school and company housing - all means of attracting as well as managing his workers. Dissenters built their own churches.

In 1824 the Government engaged Thomas Telford to design and build 32 churches and 43 manses in remote Highlands and Islands parishes: an Act of Parliament decreed that the cost per site was not to exceed £1,500. The basic design assumed a congregation of over 300; galleries could be added to increase the number to 500. Some windows were of standardized design to allow for prefabrication and economy. In those days vestries were rarely supplied for ministers, who simply walked from the manse to the church, the beadle ringing the bell as the minister approached: meanwhile the precentor had been reading the Scriptures to the waiting congregation. By 1990 only 14 of the Telford churches were still in use by the Church of Scotland, though nearly all of the manses have survived.

Within a few years of the creation of the Free Church of Scotland in 1843, no fewer than 500 Free churches were built. The Free Church, like others, provided churches for the growing urban areas. By the end of the nineteenth century, there were often several places of worship in one parish, even three or four within a stone's throw of one another. During the century the Episcopal Church, with a growing membership, built new

Not all church buildings were stone. After the Disruption the Free Church had recourse to a floating iron church which was towed by tugs up Loch Sunart to serve an area where sites for building Free Church churches were refused by landowners.

churches. For the expanding Roman Catholic population many churches - as well as homes and schools - had to be built.

More churches have been built in the twentieth century but a large number of the older ones have become redundant. Between 1929 and 1994 the number of Church of Scotland congregations fell from 2,720 to 1,639. Many former churches, therefore, mainly built from the nineteenth century onwards, survive as buildings with various uses - as theatres, community centres, museums, university lecture halls. Some are now single houses, some are blocks of flats. Likewise, many old manses are no longer occupied by ministers, but the size of their grounds (glebes) and their numerous rooms suggest family sizes, servant numbers and styles of life no longer enjoyed.

5 The Word

The Church of Rome in Scotland was replaced in 1560 by a Reformed Church approved by the Scottish Parliament. In 'The First Book of Discipline' the Scottish Reformers outlined the character of the national church which was to replace the Church of Rome. Scripture, the Reformers said, was the only authority in religion: everything not expressly commanded by the Word of God must be swept away, and the Gospel must be 'truly and openly preached in every church and assembly in the Realm'. Access to the Word, the preaching of the Word, and obedience to the Word were paramount. Every church was to be provided with a Bible in English and both Old and New Testaments were to be read through systematically at church services.

John Knox, the Reformation leader, argued that church funds should support not only the churches but also education in school and university, this in addition to the relief of the poor. Such a programme 'introduced a decided democratic tendency' says the

John Knox administering the sacrament at Calder House. Sketch by Sir David Wilkie, one of several nineteenth-century artists whose work reflected events in church history and aspects of religious life in Scotland.

church historian G D Henderson. It laid emphasis on respect for, but especially on the responsibility of, the individual - an individual who heard, understood and, it was hoped, could read the Word of God.

Local languages had been employed by the medieval Roman Church for purposes of contacting, civilizing and controlling ordinary people, but the language of religion had been Latin. The medieval Church used a Latin Bible (the Vulgate). In Scotland, as on the Continent, Latin had been the international language, the language of the church service, of officialdom and law. From the fourteenth century a form of northern English had begun to assume dominance in most parts east and south of the Highland line, also in Caithness, Orkney and Shetland. By the late fifteenth century it was called Scots. However, Scots was not to be the language in which, after the Reformation, Scottish people would have access to the Bible.

The Reformation coincided with the rapid growth of printing in Europe. The craft of printing was, and still is, central to the

The family gathered for a reading of the Bible. The Cotter's Saturday Night, *Alexander Carse.*

development of literacy. Literacy was essential to the development of the Reformation, not least in Scotland. In the fifteenth century a printing press had been set up in Mainz by Gutenberg who produced a Latin Bible, generally reckoned to be the first printed book in Europe. Walter Chepman and Andrew Myllar introduced printing to Scotland in 1507.

Parts of the Bible had been translated into English before the fifteenth century, a century during which there was determined suppression in England and Scotland of the growing number and extent of translations, John Wycliffe's being the most influential among these. William Tyndale's English translation of the New Testament was printed on the Continent in the 1520s. Merchants in St Andrews and Leith soon acquired and sold copies of this translation. After a series of attempts to counter the reforming influences from the Continent and from England, in 1543 the Scottish Parliament was persuaded to permit the reading of English and Gaelic translations of the Bible (though it was to be many years before any appeared in the latter).

> Then might have been seen the Bible lying almost upon every gentleman's table. The New Testament was borne about in many men's hands.
>
> (John Knox)

The Geneva Bible, an English version produced on the Continent by exiles from England and Scotland, was adopted as the Bible of the Reformation in Scotland. By the middle of the seventeenth century it was displaced in Scotland by the Authorized Version, first published in England in 1611. The Bible, therefore, came to Scottish people in the language, English, of a world wider than their own, but at the same time in a language more accessible to them than ever before.

Many Scots have regretted that no Bible in the Scots language was available in print at the time of, or soon after, the Reformation. In fact, there has been no translation into Scots of the complete text of the Bible, though the impressive translation of the Bible (completed in 1926) by the Scot James Moffatt bears unmistakable marks of a Scottish style of language.

Around the 1520s Murdoch Nisbet, an exiled Scot, translated the New Testament and some of the Old Testament into Scots but this was not published until 1901, having remained unknown till then except to his descendants. The first substantial printed translations into Scots of parts of the Bible appeared in the nineteenth century when Scots versions of some excerpts were commissioned from a group of Scots writers by Prince Louis Lucien Bonaparte who wished to preserve some of the languages and dialects of Europe. In 1871 the first of P Hateley Waddell's Scots translations *The Psalms frae Hebrew intil Scottis* was published, followed eight years later by *Isaiah frae Hebrew intil Scottis*. W W Smith's *New Testament in Braid Scots* was published in 1901. Scots versions of parts of the Bible were later to be produced by Thomas Whyte Paterson (Solomon), Henry Paterson Cameron (Genesis), Alex Borrowman (Ruth), and James Stuart (*Scots Gospel*). All of these were based substantially on English versions, with the exception of Waddell who used the Hebrew text. In 1983 W L Lorimer's *New Testament in Scots* was published, translated from the Greek and drawing on a wide and vigorous vocabulary of Scots words, contemporary and archaic. A great variety of imagery and vocabulary can be found in the Scots translations.

> Blessit be myld men, for thai sal weld the erde.
> Blessit be thai that murnis; for thai salbe confortit. (Nisbet)

> Happy they who are makin their maen: for they sal fin' comfort and peace.
> Happy the lowly and meek o' the yirth: for the yirth sal be their ain haddin.
> (Smith)

> How happie the dowff an dowie, for they will be comfortit!
> How happie the douce an cannie, for they will faa the yird.
> (Lorimer)

Title page of The Psalms of David, *1635.*

THE
PSALMES
of DAVID
in Profe and Meeter.

With their whole Tunes in
foure or mo parts, and
fome Pfalmes in Reports.

VVhereunto is added
many godly Prayers, and
an exact Kalendar for
XXV. yeeres to come.

Printed at EDINBURGH by the
Heires of ANDREVV HART,
ANNO DOM. 1635.

A Scots version of the Bible printed in the sixteenth century would have changed much in the character of worship and in the nature of the church in Scotland, also presumably in the general acceptance and use of the Scots language. But the Scottish Reformers depended on England for much of their support and for propaganda material. The metrical Psalms were to be in English, and the Bible in English was to be made one of the principal textbooks in Scottish schools.

Bible translation was quite different with Gaelic which as late as the eighteenth century was still spoken by about one third of the population of Scotland. The first printed book in Gaelic (1567) was a translation of Knox's *Book of Common Order* by John Carswell, Superintendent of Argyll, who recognized the need for a Gaelic Bible. The Synod of Argyll made plans for a Gaelic translation. Some Highland ministers made their own provisional translations of parts of the English Bible. It was not until the seventeenth century that an appreciable number of Gaelic Bibles was available in Scotland, in Classical Gaelic, imported from Ireland. By the end of the eighteenth century a new Scottish Gaelic Bible was under way. Its qualities of scholarship and language not only established a distinction between Scottish and Irish Gaelic, they also created some delay and defence against attempts by government and religious bodies to impose English on the Highlands.

The printing and sale of Bibles, and generous promotional activities by Bible societies, made it possible for a steadily increasing number of people to read the Scriptures by themselves. The Church ensured that the Bible was read and the Shorter Catechism taught in schools. No parents were 'suffered to neglect keeping their children at school, till they can read the Scriptures distinctly' (Synod of Glasgow and Ayr, 1700).

By the eighteenth century, Scottish households took pride in possessing their own family 'haa Bible':

The sire turns o'er, wi patriarchal grace
The big haa Bible, ance his father's pride

(Burns, 'The Cotter's Saturday Night')

By the early decades of the twentieth century virtually every school pupil in Scotland possessed or had access at home to a copy of the Authorized Version, not least for the purpose of learning passages by heart for recitation in the classroom. Towards the end of the century, however, nine English translations of the Bible were to be in regular use in Scottish churches, only fifteen per cent of the churches using the Authorized Version. The multiplicity of new translations eventually made the practice of memorizing less common, and religious education began to take many new forms which did not involve rote learning, or Bible knowledge.

These new translations also made difficult the production of a curious household item, the text box, which was to be found in evangelical households early in the twentieth century. Guests might find themselves offered the opportunity to pull out a tightly-rolled piece of paper from a large number packed into the box, or members of the family might at breakfast-time take out their text for the day, and the Word, or one verse of it, could thus be unfolded to them. The practice may be seen to have some of the qualities of a lottery, but for committed users it was but one exercise in the many Bible-centred devotions of a day.

From the Reformation onwards, the sermon - the preaching, explaining and expounding of the Word - was regarded as central in Divine Service. For some time it was a sizeable centre, often a rather weighty one. A mid-nineteenth century Free Church minister, the Rev Harry Nicoll of Auchendoir, Aberdeenshire, had a singularly stern theory of preaching. In his sermons he never told an anecdote in illustration; he never quoted poetry; he never used the first personal pronoun; he eschewed all those tricks - techniques to those who favour them - which bore the marks of emotive appeal. Contrast Mr Nicoll with 'the great Dr James Kidd' who earlier in the century had thundered with great eloquence in Aberdeen's Gilcomston Chapel, speaking out against whatever he did not like, confident that God disliked it in the same degree. Occasionally he was heard in mid-sermon to shout

'Wake up, sir! Wake up! There will no sleeping in Hell', though it might be thought that sleep would more easily have overcome Mr Nicoll's congregation. Dr Kidd cared for more than the eternal souls of his congregation. While some churchmen saw vaccination against smallpox as a sinful attempt to thwart the purposes of the Almighty, Dr Kidd, thinking better of the Almighty, lectured on the subject from the pulpit and herded scores of converts into his own house where he vaccinated them himself.

The teaching-preaching talents of Scottish ministers have inevitably varied greatly. Teaching and preaching were separated by some, the former being provided in an expository lecture after the reading: the sermon was then presented in more winning style. The Shorter Catechism argues the need for preaching:

Question 89. How is the word made effectual to salvation?

Answer. The spirit of God maketh the reading, but especially the preaching of the word, an effectual means of convincing and converting sinners...

Where people have been able to choose between places of worship, their choice has sometimes depended on the preacher as much as on any other factor. Often, too, the frequency of their attendance and the strength of their allegiance have been likewise influenced. The more conversant the listeners were with the Scriptures and with current fashions in theology or church politics, the more meticulous could be their verdicts on the preacher's performance. With the broadening of education, some congregations could fully appreciate the literary, historical and classical allusions used by preachers who resorted for illustration to the novels and biographies that were increasingly available.

The evangelical revival of the nineteenth century brought a great number of preachers to prominence. But there was scarcely a period from the Reformation until the first half of the twentieth century in which the reputation of certain Scottish preachers did not ensure that large numbers would go to hear them. The preacher's emphasis could be evangelically challenging or sternly instructive: at best it managed to be both. The sermon could have discernible shape and well-defined sequence, perhaps in the standard form of three major points or parts. Sometimes the sermon was an impassioned torrent, an avalanche, a series of extempore frantic explosions. Some people were terrified, perhaps by 'eldritch squeel an gestures' (Robert Burns), some were gently wooed into the Kingdom of God by 'an agony of earnestness', as was said of Thomas Chalmers, the Disruption leader. Terror was often precursor to wooing.

Dr Chalmers, a leading figure in the Disruption of 1843.

Sometimes sheer power of oratory, in sermon or prayer, provided for many people the uplift that for others was available in a theatre.

Religion impacted forcefully on those young people who were required at home, school or church (sometimes all three) to memorize the stern thinking, in question and answer, of the Shorter Catechism:

Question 1. What is the chief end of man?

Answer. Man's chief end is to glorify God.

This is the shortest of the 107 Answers. When the evangelist D L Moody (1837-99) addressed a gathering of children in Edinburgh he happened to ask the rhetorical question 'What is prayer?' He was astonished when hundreds of hands were raised and a chorus of voices shouted the answer to Question 98:

Answer. Prayer is an offering up of our desires unto God for things agreeable to His will, in the name of Christ, with confession of our sins, and thankful acknowledgment of his mercies.

In contrast to the Catechism the children's sermon, preached by many twentieth-century ministers, has usually made easier demands on young minds. The comparatively short, usually moralizing, children's sermon, delivered early in the morning service just before children troop off to Sunday School in the church hall, has been developed by some ministers into a minor art form, often facile, often forceful, popular with adults as with children.

It is said that the art of the great rhetorical sermon has fallen into desuetude. But there were always ministers who did not give priority - or indeed appeal - to their sermons. In *Memoirs of a Highland Lady* (1812) Elizabeth Grant of Rothiemurchus wrote of a new minister:

> Within the head was more learning than maybe half a dozen professors could boast of among them, but it was not in the divinity line...he certainly gave himself little trouble about his sermons. What he did in Gaelic I cannot say, in English he had but two, although he altered the texts to give them the air of variety: the text did not always suit the discourse but that was no matter. The semons were by no means bad, though from constant repetition they grew tiresome.

Hour glass for timing the sermon.

Sermons, from the sixteenth to the early twentieth century, might last well over an hour, some 'to be continued' at equal length later on the Sunday, some delivered in long instalments, with but one text, over several weeks. An hour glass (often a half-hour glass) stood at the side of the pulpit to let the preacher know how generously he was imparting wisdom to his flock. One minister, preaching to the Commissioners of Assembly in St Giles' Cathedral, is said to have shown neither humour nor self-knowledge when he announced before a very long sermon the text 'We have need of patience'.

Sermons, in particular those requiring patience, were part of a noteworthy sequence of developments. Beacuse so many were so long there was an increasing demand for seating. Small, portable folding stools had been used by some people, especially women: in 1604 the Kirk Session of Aberdeen ordained that all women of honest reputation who could afford stools should have them to sit on during sermons and prayers. Seats and sometimes desks were allowed for the privileged few - ladies of rank, heritors, men of quality, elders, the minister's wife and family. By the eighteenth century, pews were becoming more common and, because seats took up space, galleries or lofts were erected to accommodate more people, and where there were galleries pulpits had to be raised so that the minister could be heard by all, sounding boards then ensuring that all downstairs could hear too. Seat rents were charged, loft seats going to the highest bidder. Lairds had their own well-appointed and decorated lofts.

At the beginning of the nineteenth century heritors were obliged to provide adequate seating spaces, eighteen by 29 inches per posterior, for their parishioners. In turn the arrival of pews hampered the customary observance of Communion at long central tables, so began the service of Communion to pews, and then the provision of small glasses for the wine. Cushions added comfort to the pews. As for warmth, coal fires were attempted, but a packed congregation could create its own warmth, and ventilation became a problem. Staying awake or sitting attentively through a long sermon could be difficult, especially for children. The endurance test was made easier by refreshment. Sermons were even timed by the pandrop (a mint imperial), 'twa pandrops, weel sookit an nae crunchit' being adjudged the limit.

Church in Traquhair showing the outside stair to the laird's loft. SLA

The popular appeal which sermons have at times enjoyed is seen in the sales achieved by volumes of sermons. Hazlitt reported how some of Thomas Chalmers's sermons 'ran like wildfire through the country, were the darlings of watering places, were laid in the windows of inns, and were to be met with in all places of public resort'. When the Rev John Caird preached before Queen Victoria at Crathie Church a sermon on 'Religion in common life', the Queen demanded its publication. It went through many editions and was widely translated. It is claimed that sermons were at that time the most popular form of reading material in Scotland. Preaching aids abounded in print, as did inspirational, moralizing material in periodicals and novels.

Heated controversy often focused on whether a preacher used 'the paper', as the written sermon was sometimes contemptuously called. Stories are told of how ministers disguised the fact that they were reading sermons, for instance by hiding the pages of a sermon within the pulpit Bible - not easy if a gallery overlooked the pulpit. One minister, it was rumoured, wrote his notes large so that he could place them on the pulpit floor and read them. The touring evangelist or the popular guest minister had less of a problem, for the same sermon, soon committed to memory, could be delivered many times. Sermon addicts welcomed the opportunity to hear again a particular sermon by an eminent preacher.

Ministers who read their prayers were criticized almost as often as those who read their sermons - almost, because worshippers were usually expected to have their eyes closed during prayer. The proprieties of prayerful postures have varied over the years, and from one denomination to another. Congregations have knelt, sat and stood, one determinant having been the appropriateness of church furniture. Commissioners at the Church of Scotland General Assembly stand for prayer, though few do so in church. (Equally varied as postures for prayer have been habits of headwear for both men and women, whether on or off.)

The attitudes of Scots people to formal prayers may have been unduly coloured or distorted by the legend of Jenny Geddes. She is said to have thrown her stool (an item of personal, portable furniture of the time, 1637) at the clergyman in St Giles' Cathedral who attempted to read from a new Prayer Book which King Charles I was trying to impose, without consultation, on the Scottish Church. A riot ensued. The Reformation, however, had not brought immediate or strong opposition to commonly agreed formality in prayer, or to prescribed forms of expression. The Lord's Prayer, the Apostles' Creed and the Ten Commandments were repeated at post-Reformation services. Eventually the Lord's Prayer suffered neglect by those who argued against 'vain repetition' by minister or congregation, an attitude that prevailed well into the twentieth century. In the mid-nineteenth century a movement began in Scotland in favour of increased ritual, but simplicity in services and distinctively personal styles in prayer have prevailed in many churches.

Probably more anecdotes centre on Scots ministers' and elders' prayers than on any other aspect of Scottish church practice, and many of the stories tell of the extempore individual touch. One Cromarty elder, praying about the vine and the branches, became so enthused about the subject that he cried 'Dig about us and dung us, Lord !' Imagery just as homely was achieved by the minister who addressed his Maker: 'Thou, O Lord, art like a mouse in a dry-stane dyke - aye keekin' oot at us frae holes an crannies. But we cannae see Thee.' Prayer in church can become a multi-purpose and multi-directional exercise, the pulpit tending to become a point halfway between Man and his Maker, the minister as likely to pray at as for his flock. The renowned divinity professor Dr John Duncan (1796-1870) was critical of ministers: 'We have far too many preaching prayers; many good ministers preach to God.' Some ministers are more tutor than preacher - of the kind novelist Ian Hay describes, who prayed for that 'adjacent kingdom of England which, as Thou knowest, Oh Lord, lies to the south of Scotland'.

None of which should be taken to suggest that prayer has not been seen as a very serious matter, usually a dignified, often a most moving part of church worship. Prayers may relate closely to contemporary events, local needs and national politics, sometimes national grief, also national remembrance. Prayer can be part of a pleasing social convention. The words of some prayers are known to many and uttered in all manner of settings, like the family grace at table, or the best-known Scottish grace:

> Some hae meat, and cannae eat,
> And some wad eat that want it;
> But we hae meat, and we can eat,
> And sae the Lord be thankit.

Prayers may be sung, and have been for centuries. Prayer in large gatherings, as in privacy, may be silent. Perhaps the proverb 'There is no wisdom like silence' has been too often disregarded. Not by Quakers, for whom silence is central element of worship.

6 The song

St Columba is said to have produced a book of hymns for the seven days of the week and to have had a remarkable singing voice, like a melodious lion, both powerful and compelling. The themes of some hymns in use today are attributed to him, for example:

> O God, Thou art the Father
> Of all that have believed . . .

and:

> Alone with none but Thee, my God
> I journey on my way. . .

Chants honouring St Columba were probably being sung from the seventh century onwards. By the thirteenth century there were some sizeable ecclesiastical centres in Scotland (eg Holyrood, Glasgow, Dunkeld, St Andrews, Elgin, Aberdeen, Kirkwall) where musical resources and activities were significant. Larger churches allowed for more impressive sounds, and the music in the Mass was now enriched by instrumental accompaniment and by choirs singing in harmony as well as unison.

Sang Schules (Song Schools) were established in cathedrals, monasteries and parish churches from Kirkwall to Melrose. Music had to be written and choirs trained. Singing clergy and boys in the Sang Schules acquired musical literacy. But understanding of the words that were sung, mostly from the Book of Psalms, was limited to those who knew Latin, and much of the music may have had little appeal for the untutored ear.

Away from the churches, people were learning to sing words they understood to simple and memorable melodies. The words had rhythm and rhyme - and were often improper. In the 1540s John Wedderburn, of Dundee, decided to convert the bawdy verses into godly ones. A number of the verses in his *Gude and Godlie Ballatis* were versions of the Psalms which soon became popular, though they were not sung in public services. Some of his Ballads were defamatory of church and churchmen and so were outlawed for several years. These Ballads as a whole are lar exuli uelut sydus p seculi fide pces uo ipsm xpm ducit ad gaudia. euo

Pastor oues ppriis humeris ad ouile reportes. digneris supis nos sociair

euoü. Freptus pcibus ad festa supna notatos. attrahe nos famulos scd

mos. euoü. Psallat ergo sedule suo grex pastori. luiger p brauio ps u

choru ne si in hoc stadio pmittamur mori p nobis suggerito pri plasm

euoü. Tuis pri laudibs laxet chorus loza sic totis ympnidicis concio

na p tua menta credimus saluari p3 fata laucrea reati; reari. euoü. Mes

Occliurin insignis signifer. mentes munda ne falleris pestifer serius offi

ma ns discrimine. Tuis ut placeat exgiditis psallere. Tibi pie cetus co

pme notes letare. hut aure adhibe tuis. Glia pri x filio x spiritui sco.

Saluator pissime columba cuius ortum repli pmostrarut angelici believed to have helped attune Scottish minds to the principles of the Reformation, and the psalm-versions probably led to the early acceptance by Scots of the metrical psalms in the First Scottish Psalter of 1564. Reformation thinking favoured a simple and pure singing of divine praise by people who understood the words they sang, so choral works with Latin wording and the use of musical instruments were generally abandoned as part of church worship. John Knox accepted the view of Calvin that only what was biblical should be used in public worship. The hymns of the Roman church were set aside, the Old Testament Psalms providing the only wording for sung worship. So for about three centuries most church people in Scotland were to sing only pre-Christian verses of praise.

The 1564 Psalter, drawing on psalters produced on the Continent and in England, contained metrical psalms, words by both English and Scots versifiers (though not in the Scots language), with tunes from a variety of sources - German, French, English and Scottish. It was well into the seventeenth century before harmonized versions of the tunes were printed in Scotland. The psalms were not printed in metre in Gaelic until 1659, so till then Highlanders could acquire the tunes only by oral transmission, in which process the tunes were adjusted to the Highland idiom, with grace-notes and variations in abundance.

In the early years of the Reformation the title 'Uptaker of the Psalms' was given to the leader of the singing in public worship; he was usually also the Reader (of Scriptures) or Lettergae, his desk being the lectern or letteran. The term Precentor came into use in the seventeenth century, about the same time as proposals from the Westminster Assembly (1643) were put into practice 'that for the present, where many of the congregation cannot read, it is convenient that the minister or some other fit person appointed by him and the other ruling officers do read the

Inchcolm Antiphoner, late thirteenth or early fourteenth century, containing remnants of Celtic church music in Scotland.

psalm, line by line, before the singing thereof'. Many Scots thought the proposal an insult to their superior education. In 1746 the Church of Scotland General Assembly recommended that schoolmasters (who were often the precentors) should instruct pupils in singing the common psalm-tunes, and that 'reading the line' should end. However, the practice was stubbornly retained by some who had come to regard it as a heritage to be dearly prized. Precentors continued as leaders of worship until they were replaced by musical instruments and choirs. Precentors' desks, placed below or near the pulpit, were still being installed in new churches in the nineteenth century. Today precentors still lead unaccompanied singing in Free and Free Presbyterian churches.

The Second Psalter, which came into use in 1650, contained no tunes. In 1666 the Aberdeen Psalter appeared and contained only twelve common-metre tunes. Under what has been called the Tyranny of the Twelve Tunes the musical repertory for most Scots congregations was sadly limited for many years. Church singing has often suffered from religious zeal which has not been matched by musical talent or training. Elizabeth Grant of Rothiemurchus (1812) recorded:

> serious severe screaming quite beyond the natural pitch of the voice, a wandering search after the air by many who never caught it, a flourish of difficult execution and plenty of the 'tremolo' lately come into fashion. The dogs seized this occasion to bark (for they always came to the kirk with the family) and the babies to cry.

Another Grant, Sir Archibald Grant of Monymusk, had begun to set things right in the middle of the eighteenth century in Aberdeenshire. He ran choir practices in his library, accompanied by an organ. He recruited an English private soldier stationed in Aberdeen, Thomas Channon, who was obligingly discharged

A musician depicted in An Account of the Scottish Psalter of AD 1566.

It may be knawn be my hewinly hew

I ā ane mā of mekill modestie

And pairfor syngis my part w' notis
most trew.

As it efferis vnto my facultie.

TENNOWR.

from the army. Soon Channon was training local choirs in three-and four-part harmony and in precise timing. He also introduced new psalm tunes and anthems. He used a pitch-pipe for precision in key, a 'profane practice' condemned as singing the sacred psalms with a herd-boy's whistle. Nevertheless the choir movement had begun. Edinburgh, Dundee and Glasgow followed suit.

A stern reverence for the Bible, including the metrical psalms, prevailed so that even to use the words of psalms in singing practice was thought irreverent. However, the tunes were not thought sacrosanct. So new words were set to the tunes, pious and moralizing at first, then less reverent.

> How lovely is thy dwelling place,
> Sir Archie Grant to me;
> The home-park and the policies,
> How pleasant, sir, they be.

Young people of both sexes gathered for choir practice on week-nights, and they sat together during the Sunday service, sometimes in a choir loft. Here was a new social activity and focus in church life. The practice verses spread from district to district, boys and girls chanted them as they walked home together. Some verses were repeated *sotto voce* in church.

Poets in England and Scotland were asked to produce paraphrases in common metre of Old and New Testament passages. When a collection of these was produced in 1781 they were resisted by some churchmen as being too evangelical. But Scottish Presbyterians could not isolate themselves for long either from external religious influence or from the new and fast-spreading interest in music, folk and classical, among Scots people at that time.

The evangelical revival which originated in England in the eighteenth century had stimulated demand for joyful hymns and livelier tunes. In 1786 the first Scottish Presbyterian hymn book was published, by James Steuart of Anderston Relief Church,

Glasgow. The United Presbyterian Church produced a hymn book in 1852. The Church of Scotland's *Scottish Hymnal* arrived in 1870, followed by a Free Church hymn book in 1873. Then all three agreed on the *Scottish Church Hymnary* of 1898. A new edition appeared in 1927 and a further one in 1973.

In the 1850s came a second evangelical revival. Evangelists and mission preachers visited towns and villages, drawing some people from, and feeding some to, the churches. D L Moody, the American evangelist and hymn-writer, came first to Scotland with Ira D Sankey in 1873. Over the next 20 years Moody's preaching, Sankey's singing (to organ accompaniment) and their hymns brought new religious zeal to many, stimulating new approaches to worship, to preaching, to theology and to the role of lay people in church affairs. Where hymns were still not sung in churches, many people sang from the Moody and Sankey hymn-book in their own homes. Some in the Highlands held their own hymn ceilidhs. Also to Moody and Sankey must go credit for a widespread acceptance of the organ in church music and in people's homes.

It is thought likely that a kind of organ was being used in Scotland in the twelfth century. Bells had been the earliest musical instruments associated with Christianity (St Mungo's bell appears on Glasgow's coat of arms). Bells were thought to have healing

Hymn boards from Monzie Kirk, Perthshire.

powers. They were useful, too, for telling people the time. By the end of the seventeenth century St Giles' Cathedral in Edinburgh had a 21-bell carillon on which were played 'all manner of tunes' to the delight of the citizens, though a less joyous mood on one occasion is recorded: in 1707 on the day of the Union of the Scottish and English parliaments the carilloner played 'Why should I be sad on my wedding day?' St Giles' bells were removed in the early twentieth century, but there are still 50 carillons in Scotland, six full ones (minimum of 23 bells) and 44 part ones. Those in St Nicholas, Aberdeen, and St John's, Perth, are among the best known. Most church bells strike the time or call people to worship with a comparatively limited melody. The single church bell was for some time used to punctuate certain stages in the progress of worship. Much less common in today's churches is the harp or clarsach, in the early days of Christianity said to be the proper instrument for praising God.

Simple pipes and horns belong to pre-Christian times, and the monocordis, a simple keyboard instrument, appeared in fifteenth-century Scotland. The technical development from these three, the organ, has a chequered history in the Scottish church. Reformation thinking argued that all parts of worship must be authorized by New Testament example, so instrumental music was excluded. Church organs were destroyed or removed. The precentor then dominated Presbyterian church music for more than 200 years.

In the 1720s an organ was installed in St Paul's Episcopal Chapel in Aberdeen, the first in a public Scottish church since the Reformation. Organs were then provided in other Episcopalian and non-Presbyterian churches in the course of the eighteenth century, most of the organists, indeed most of the men bringing new life to Scottish music, coming from England. An attempt was made in 1807 to introduce an organ (constructed by James Watt)

Ninian, believed to have been the earliest Christian missionary to Scotland.

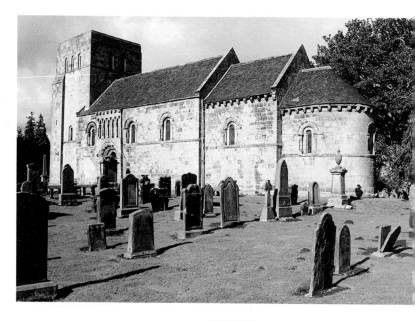

Dalmeny, st Cuthbert's Church, near Edinburgh, is thought to retain more of the original medieval church building than any of the other ancient churches still used by the Church of Scotland. Anne Maxwell

The mask of the Rev Alexander Peden, Covenanting Minister, late 17th century.

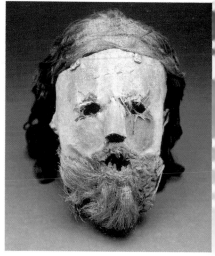

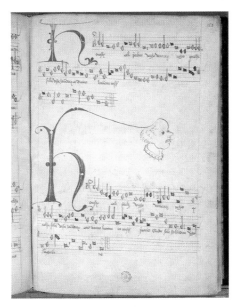

Carver choirbook, seventeenth century. This manuscript is named after the the sixteenth-century composer Robert Carver because it contains many of his compositions, including the polyphonic settings of the Mass.

Greyfriars Kirk, Edinburgh. John Elphinstone.

George Wishart
Preaching against
Idolatry *by Fettes
Douglas, 1871. Wishart
(about 1513-46) was
charged with heresy,
left Scotland, but
returned and preached
widely before being
arrested and burned at
St Andrews.*

*Stobo Kirk painted by
James McIntosh
Patrick in 1936.*

to St Andrew's Parish Church in Glasgow, but its music was heard for only one day. In the 1820s a Glasgow minister, Dr William Anderson, produced a pamphlet ridiculing the arguments then being advanced against the introduction of organs. In 1856 Claremont United Presbyterian Church, Glasgow, installed an organ but was not allowed to use it until 1872. But worship reform in Scotland was growing apace. John Curwen's Tonic Sol-Fa system was introduced into choir training around this time. Dr Robert Lee of Old Greyfriars, Edinburgh, made a variety of controversial and much publicized innovations in worship, including a harmonium and then an organ. The 'kist o whistles', as the organ was called by some, was widely accepted in the Church of Scotland by the 1870s. Resistance lasted longer in the Free Church and has been maintained by the smaller group of Free churches (Wee Frees) who stayed outside the union of Free and UP churches in 1900.

The swing in favour of organs was encouraged greatly by grants from Andrew Carnegie (1835-1919) for the purchase of organs. It had one remarkable, indeed regrettable, effect, taking place as it did when, because of population growth and movement and also denominational fervour, an unprecedented number of churches were being built or renovated. In many churches the new organ became the central architectural feature, its rows of large pipes arrayed above and around the pulpit. The organ console was used in some churches as the communion table, and the dominant effect was of concert-hall rather than church, especially when a sizeable choir was assembled round the console.

Country churches usually had to be content with small organs, some of which were powered by hand-operated bellows. Others had a foot-bellows harmonium, an instrument at one stage installed in a number of homes where hymn-singing was popular. In the late twentieth century electric organs have been introduced to many churches. Guitars and synthesizers have been thought appropriate for attracting the young. In some churches, partly because of the shortage of money, a form of karaoke has been employed, the requisite tapes being purchased from North America, where the practice is gaining in popularity.

Most of the comparatively few hymns written by Scots belong to the nineteenth century. The best-known among them include 'O worship the King, all glorious above' (Sir Robert Grant 1779-1838), 'Jesus, tender Shepherd, hear me' (Mary Lundie Duncan 1814-40), 'Come, children, join to sing' (Christian Henry Bateman 1813-89), and 'We plough the fields and scatter' (Jane Montgomery Campbell 1817-78). Four Church of Scotland minister-hymnwriters deserve special mention. Prominent in Scottish church life, and expressing strong personal beliefs and feelings, in their hymns they mirrored contemporary religious concepts and they gave churchfolk words that could be sung with vigour and conviction. Norman MacLeod (1712-72) wrote 'Courage, Brother, do not stumble'; George Matheson (1842-1906) 'O Love that wilt not let me go'; Lachlan MacLean Watt (1867-1957) 'O Thou my Judge and King'. Duncan MacGregor (1854-1923) argued in his writings that the liturgy of early worship in Scotland had been markedly rich. In translating Columba's 'O God Thou art the Father' he was bridging thirteen centuries of Christian belief - and song.

7 On the Sabbath

John Knox had argued for a school in every parish, to teach at least the reading-literacy needed for the study of the Bible. By the late eighteenth and early nineteenth century the level and range of education in Scotland were in most respects greater than in England. But it was in England, in the late eighteenth century, that Sunday Schools originated, for the benefit of those children who were working six days a week. On Sunday, the one day off granted to most working children, Sunday classes in reading, writing and arithmetic, plus of course Bible knowledge, were provided. These Sunday Schools were approved by some people as means of keeping the children off the streets; by others they were seen as giving the youngsters ideas above their station. The innovation soon spread northward and Sunday Schools were being organized, often with paid teachers, in Edinburgh, Glasgow, Aberdeen and other centres by the last years of the eighteenth century. The brothers Robert and James Haldane, philanthropists and itinerant evangelists, brought a more vigorously evangelical note, as well as considerable funding, to their concept of Sunday (or Sabbath) Schools, many of these manned by unpaid volunteers.

In the course of the nineteenth century, Ragged (and Industrial) Schools were set up in Scotland, providing food, clothing and instruction for vagrant children. But by the 1840s Sunday Schools, essentially for religious instruction and for all kinds of children, were widespread, not least in the new Free Church of Scotland. By the end of the century Sunday Schools were central to church life and many children attended regularly while their parents seldom or never made an appearance. But it was hoped that such provision for children (followed as the children grew older by Bible Class, and accompanied by access to youth organizations such as the Boys' Brigade, which began in Glasgow in 1883) would ensure adult church membership in later years.

Recruitment to Sunday School teaching was also a means of confirming - for many, enriching - church membership. There are no reliable statistics to show the numbers of young people engaged in Sunday education of one kind and another by the end of the nineteenth century. One mission hall alone, in Aberdeen, had an average attendance of about 250 at its Sunday School. Attendance at some Sunday Schools could vary depending on the approach of the Christmas treat or the annual picnic outing in the summer. In *Farmer's Boy* John R Allan approached the Sunday School experience with more humour than reverence:

> Mr Amos Black...had a high Roman nose through which he used to intone God's mercy in a cross between the Anglican whine and the Presbyterian snarl. I disliked his religion, which was too full of

*Early twentieth-century Sunday School outing in Fife,
taking refuge from the rain.* SLA

prohibitions, but I am sure he was a really good man and sincere
in his beliefs. At any rate he was kinder than the God he preached,
for he always had a pocketful of pandrops which he doled out to us
before he began his exposition of the golden text... The proceed-
ings opened with a hymn, one of those maudlin things written for
and despised by children. Then Mr Black clasped his hands where
his stomach ought to have been in a man of his age, closed his eyes
and, elevating his trumpet nose, told the Lord that we were little
children weak in everything but original sin.

An Aberdeen girl, Isabella Morrice, a shoemaker's daughter, was
to write of Sundays in the 1890s:

We never thought of not going to church and we loved the Sunday
School (on Sunday afternoon). Going to church was a family affair,
we all went and all our chums went to Sunday School. We were
expected to remember the text when we got home and to be able to

tell what the Sunday School lesson was about. It was excellent training in concentration. Moreover there was the pleasure of seeing all our friends and acquaintances in their Sunday best. We not only had a special dress for Sundays but our underclothing, shoes, stockings and hat were all sacred to Sunday. On one occasion only was the Sunday dress worn on a weekday and that was at the yearly school examination. 'Be sure to have on your Sunday dresses', the teacher said. There was also a Bible examination but for that we only got a new pinafore. Some children we knew of put pinafores over their Sunday dresses when they sat down to dinner but that was slovenly and lazy and in our house the dress had to be changed, and then changed again for Sunday School. It was a wonderful thought that next year this grandeur would be worn to school.

Your Father and I

Isabella Morrice wrote, too, of Sunday afternoon set aside for inspirational reading. Thus she came to know *Pilgrim's Progress* almost by heart. For such Sabbath leisure reading, worthy family magazines were published and became available in bound volumes, for example *The Sunday at Home; for Sabbath Reading* issued by the London Religious Tract Society. The print was small and densely presented on the pages of the magazine, with occasional illustrations.

In the early days of the Christian Church in Scotland the belief that the Lord's Day must be set aside for the worship of God and for rest, and that all work and travel were prohibited, clearly introduced some degree of protection for the lower orders. The same protection continued until the sixteenth century when the Sabbath was still widely though not relentlessly observed. Attendance at church on the Sabbath was seen by the Reformed church as a weekly public engagement reflecting, it was hoped, the daily private practice of family worship.

In the course of the seventeenth century Scottish Presbyterians became markedly severe with Sabbath-breaking backsliders. The so-called '24-hour Sabbath' came into being. For serious offences in those days offenders might be 'confined to the

Stool of repentance for parish transgressors.

jougs' (iron collars fixed to the church gate or to a wall in the church) or fined - the proceeds usually going to the poor of the parish. Profaning of the Sabbath was likely to require the offender to stand at the stool of repentance, or 'cutty stool', usually placed near the pulpit.

Modes of inquisition which had been adopted by seventeenth- and eighteenth-century kirk sessions in dealing with scandals were documented in the 1880s by Andrew Edgar, minister of Mauchline, Ayrshire (where Mr Auld, of Burns fame, had held sway). Sabbath-breaking was a scandal, as were insolence to or slanders of any member of the kirk session, drunkenness, broils and bickering, theft, murder, impurity, witchcraft, cursing, heresy and so on. Breach of the Sabbath figured most prominently, 'next to impurity', among common offences. Sunday offences listed by Edgar included absence from church; 'playing at pennystone' (1670); 'bringing home herring'; 'travelling to Glasgow and bringing a cow from Eaglesham' (1675); one person providing, another accepting the services of a barber (1780); 'idly vaguing together'; 'profane worldly conversation' (1786). Two interesting eighteenth-century cases relate to people ineptly versed in the calendar, who did not know it was Sunday - 'the kirk session held it inexcusable that any person should not know Sunday from Saturday'. For such offences punishments included: 'minister instructed to speak to him'; 'to sign a bond'; public rebuke.

Severity towards Sabbath-breakers was relaxed by some churches in the eighteenth century. The resurgence of evangelism is credited with, or blamed for, a marked tightening of attitude in the course of the nineteenth century. In 1831 John MacMaster, probationer, eloped with a lady. As if that were not bad enough he committed this 'gross profanation' on the Sabbath 'under cloud of night'. He was deposed.

In the mid-nineteenth century an intense debate centred on the subject of rail travel which was then spreading fast. In the Church of Scotland and the Free Church, ministers were admonished for suggesting any degree of tolerance towards the provision or use of rail transport on Sundays. In 1847 the Sabbath Alliance was founded, largely under Free Church auspices. In 1863 the Free Church Glasgow Presbytery instructed the removal of the name of James Robertson, a *Glasgow Herald* compositor, from the

Outdoors church service at Lochcarron, Wester Ross, early twentieth century. Part of the congregation left the Free Church in 1905. Excluded from using the parent church building, they held services outdoors until, as a part of the United Free Church, a new church could be constructed. SLA

Communion roll of a Gorbals congregation because he worked on the Sabbath.

Attitudes to the Sabbath have varied markedly between the denominations, also within these, and remnants of the differences have continued, not least in relation to conditions of employment, availability of public transport and of entertainment. Churchmen, especially Catholics, encouraged the playing of football as a healthy sport for boys and men who were required to work in deplorable industrial settings. But by the early twentieth century the game was fast becoming professional and was seen by sterner churchmen almost as a rival religion, dominating Saturday activity and preoccupying Sunday thought. Later in the century sports of all kinds were to be played on the Sabbath.

In the history of Sabbath observance there are many recurring themes, protection not the least of them. In the fast-growing overcrowded cities of the nineteenth century it was reasonable that churchmen, still accepting social duties and roles of influence and oversight, would try to protect people from all those who wished to exploit them. In 1849 the Rev R H Muir, Dalmeny, presented to the General Assembly of the Church of Scotland a report of the Temperance Committee detailing numbers of public houses, their opening on Sundays, the payment of wages across bars, the temptations of feeing markets, the iniquities of the bothy system and so on. On one Sunday in Edinburgh, it was found, 4,631 children under 14 and 3,032 under eight were seen to enter public houses. The challenge of alcohol was the first thing that brought together the deeply divided Scottish churches, and together they had a commendable degree of success in ensuring that some excesses and social outrages were reduced. Sabbatarian arguments were deployed by the churches in effecting the necessary legislation by Parliament. However, the resulting Act in 1853 could not by itself turn people from licensed houses to the House of God. At that time about a fifth of the population attended church: as ever, a much larger number claimed church connection of some kind.

8 Belonging

The concept of belonging to a church, to a religious denomination or congregation, has changed over the years, often depending on who had reason to believe that the church, or part of it, belonged to them. Up to the twentieth century, landowners (or heritors) were required to provide and maintain parish churches and church grounds. In the 1820s, for example, the Duke of Atholl, Mr McInroy of Lude Estate, and Robertson of Struan contributed 63 per cent, sixteen per cent and six per cent of the £1,039 needed to build the new Blair Atholl Church, the Duke donating an acre of ground around the church to be used as burial ground, all timber for the church to come from Atholl plantations. The landowners' contributions were in proportion to the rents from their estates; their seat entitlements accordingly being 368, 96 and 37. The Duke was to have a pew in front of his own

Certificate of worthiness to join 'any Christian congregation'
issued to Janet Black of Inveresk in 1790.

entrance to the church, the pew to be panelled, with a cornice and architrave moulding round the arch above. The Duke's workers also had the right to use his entrance to the church.

In the mid-nineteenth century, when the number of Episcopalians in Scotland was increasing, the money required for the building of St John's Episcopal Church, Edinburgh, was raised partly by donations and partly by loans which brought the lenders three per cent dividends. Investment in church building, again not necessarily by church members, had been common in seceding churches and also for new building by the Church of Scotland, for which town councils provided some funding. Seat rents then had to be sufficiently high to ensure repayment or payment of appropriate interest. Seat rents, which had become possible only in the eighteenth century when fixed seats were introduced, became a principal means of building and maintaining churches. They could also contribute to the building of mission churches for the poor and to the development of foreign missions.

Those wealthy enough to pay high seat rents inevitably gained personal status within their congregation and their community, the community being perhaps that of a dominant city church or

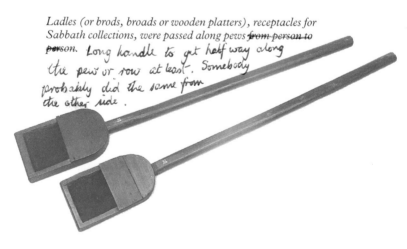

Ladles (or brods, broads or wooden platters), receptacles for Sabbath collections, were passed along pews ~~from person to person.~~ Long handle to get half way along the pew or row at least. Somebody probably did the same from the other side.

of a new upper-class suburban one. The new Free Church drew an appreciable amount of its funds from the new, upwardly mobile moneyed middle classes of the mid-nineteenth century, people who had come out against patronage but then themselves became patrons of a kind. Some less wealthy Free churchmen had merely contributed by helping with the physical building of their new church. In many different ways people belonged to churches that belonged to them. In the early twentieth century visitors to Edinburgh could find themselves held back at the door of St Giles' Cathedral until a few minutes before the service was due to begin: it was assumed that pew holders were by then in place so the outsiders were allowed to fill vacant seats. By the middle of the century seat renting in Scottish churches was a thing of the past.

The story of nineteenth-century Scotland tells of countless people for whom both commitment and the freedom to change were essential ingredients of religious life. The Rev Donald Sage (1789-1869) telling of his student days, wrote:

> Brown, my landlord, could not be curbed within the limits
> of any particular sect, but on the contrary was continually wan-
> dering from chapel to chapel, and from one sect to another.

In so far as religion was fashionable in nineteenth-century Scotland there was a strong note of competition in its observance. A variety of institutions were ready or would arise to cater for the competition. From the 1843 Disruption stemmed the greatest activity. Smaller and independent denominations were gaining in strength. William Booth came to win souls in Scotland in 1869: in 1879 the first Scottish corps of his Salvation Army was established in Anderston, Glasgow. The vigour of the Army's evangelism was matched by its courageous welfare work with the destitute and its extensive work as an emigration agency. The Brethren, too, had sprung to life in 1827, and thereafter in their various groups distinguished themselves for their capacity now to hold together and now to fall apart. Missions sprang up here and there for the purpose of turning people to the churches, though some were to become separate sects: they ran tent meetings and distributed tracts. They missed no opportunity for evangelism. They looked on the annual Highland Show as yet another field to be ploughed for the Master, and they ran penny deposit banks for the poor.

Some people have established a sense of belonging by attaching themselves to small, rebel or schismatic groups, others by becoming part of the largest organization they can find. The Christian Church today embraces both of these attitudes. Within most Scottish churches of the late nineteenth and early twentieth centuries diverse factors contributed to a sense of belonging. Members were encouraged to think of the Christian Church as a proudly historic church. The main Christian churches, however separated, were seen both as national and as strongly local churches. Increasing numbers of memorial plaques to local men who had died serving their nation appeared on church walls. Acceptance of churches as centres of the community is still apparent in events such as annual services of remembrance and thanksgiving, or the kirking of a council (usually in a long- established city church), this when councillors from several denominations or from none process for the occasion. Likewise the celebration of centenaries by national or international associations. Mauchline elders of the late eighteenth century would scarcely have believed it possible that the Burns Federation and many others would process to a St Giles' Cathedral service in 1996 to mark the two hundredth anniversary of Burns's death.

In his time Burns mocked many of the doctrines and practices of the Church and churchmen:

> O Thou that in the Heavens does dwell
> Wha, as it pleases best Thysel
> Sends ane to Heaven an ten to Hell,
>> Aa for Thy glory
> And no for onie guid or ill
>> They've done before Thee !
>
> ('Holy Willie's Prayer')

For many people doctrines of Predestination and Election were scarcely conducive to a secure sense of belonging. A number of churchmen set out to present Christianity in a more acceptable light. Among these was John McLeod Campbell (1800-72) of Rhu, Dunbartonshire. He was deposed for heresy by the General Assembly in 1831 because he preached Universal Atonement, saying that pardon for sins was free to all men and that Christ had atoned fully. His beliefs, which gained support among churchmen through the remainder of the century, effectively undermined the idea of Christ dying for only a mysteriously chosen Elect.

Conflict among Scottish churchmen was equally intense later in the century on the subject of the literal and historical authenticity of the Bible. This controversy centred at one point on Professor William Robertson Smith (1846-94). In an article entitled 'Bible' in the *Encyclopedia Britannica* (1875) he dared to present arguments, then gaining currency among academics, which were seen to undermine long-held beliefs in how the Bible should be interpreted. In 1881 he was dismissed from his chair in Aberdeen's Free Church College but allowed to remain a minister: he could preach but not teach. The 'higher criticism' of Smith and other scholars was attacked for endangering the stability of people's Christian faith. It distressed and divided ministers and churchgoers. It required them to take sides in arguments that many did not understand.

Nearer the understanding of the ordinary churchgoer, and more ameliorative in effect, were the writings of George MacDonald (1826-1905). As preacher, poet and novelist he dared to argue that some provision was made for the heathen after death and that God's love was for all:

> I did not care for God to love me if He did not love everybody: the kind of love I needed was the love that all men needed, the love that belonged to their nature as the children of the Father.

MacDonald has been described as the first distinctively Scottish writer to popularize the idea of God's Fatherhood. Such thinking led churchgoers to see themselves as belonging to the family of God. And the main churches of the nineteenth century aimed to extend that family. They were active missionary churches. When congregations sang Charles Wesley's 'Come thou long-expected Jesus' they asserted that He was the 'Dear Desire of every nation'. A large number of the first women to qualify in medicine went into the mission field. Scottish missionaries - some known by the name of their mission field (Mary Slessor of Calabar, Graham of Kalimpong) - returned on leave to preach to the folk at home. On furlough, Mary Slessor (1848-1915) gained notice for her cause by bringing with her some of the African children she had adopted. Some missionaries gave lantern lectures showing mission work in all parts of the Empire and beyond. A 1930s advertisement offered:

> Unit Portable Lantern. Light, Unbreakable, Non-inflammable. The ideal instrument for Church work, especially in scattered parishes. Used by the Church of Scotland Home Department, Foreign Missions, Women's Temperance Association etc

As the Church lost direct control of religious instruction in schools it devoted new resources to the work of Sunday Schools, Bible Classes and Youth Fellowships. The new church halls of the early twentieth century served the purposes not only of prayer meetings but also of various youth movements, of Women's Guilds, of social functions and sales of work. Some churches built in new housing areas after the Second World War were deliberately constructed to serve as both church and social centre, dimensions even calculated to ensure accommodation of a badminton court, and provision being made for sanctuary space to be screened off - almost reverting to medieval church practice. Nurseries, playgroups and so on were welcomed. Then questions arose about whether political meetings or social gatherings, possibly with questionable entertainment, should be allowed.

Commercial entertainment has offered people alternatives to many church-centred activities. But allegiance to or at least

*Twentieth-century Sunday School picnic at Muckhart,
Perthshire.* SLA

attendance at churches has been sustained in part by those services which churches provide to mark important family events -
baptisms, weddings, funerals. Some people have maintained
the formality of church membership by occasionally attending
Communion.

9 Occasions

Gordon Donaldson, H M Historiographer in Scotland, wrote
(1990) that as a result of the Reformation:

> many must have felt that with the suppression of the Latin rite
> and the erosion of belief in the sacrificial character of the Eucharist,
> something which for centuries had nourished the devotion of
> the saints and countless other Christians, was being abruptly
> discarded.

This, he suggested, was the biggest breach in the history of Scottish Christianity. The sacrament of Holy Communion, however, in one form or another, has been and still is, central to the life of nearly all Christian churches. In medieval times the doctrine of transubstantiation was developed, affirming that in the Eucharist (or Mass or Holy Communion or Lord's Supper) the bread and wine were changed into the substance of the body and blood of Christ. Knox and other Scots Protestants were determined to counter this doctrine. Some questioned, among other things, the Romish practice of kneeling at Communion (they thought the worship of a wafer was idolatrous). They wished, however, to retain Communion as a regular act of communal worship to which all who had been baptized and who continued in the faith were welcomed. In the nineteenth century, ceremonies of confirmation were instituted for admitting those who had been baptized to participate in Communion.

Soon after the Reformation tokens, or tickets, were issued as means of admission to Communion. The tokens, often metal, produced in a variety of shapes and with inscriptions usually showing the name of the church, sometimes carried the Bible

Communion token and the mould in which it was made.

reference I Corinthians XI, 28, 29 which reads:

> But let a man examine himself, and so let him eat of that bread,
> and drink of that cup, For he that eateth and drinketh unworthily,
> eateth and drinketh damnation to himself, not discerning
> the Lord's body.

Not an openly welcoming declaration. As far back as the eleventh
century Queen Margaret had questioned the exclusiveness of St
Paul's words. They were, however, used until the twentieth
century by some Presbyterian churches as justification for the
custom of 'fencing the tables', excluding those who thought
themselves unworthy or who, as a matter of church discipline,
were deemed unfit to participate. Latterly, printed tickets have
been distributed for collection at Communion, as a means of
checking at least some level of attendance.

In 'The Holy Fair' Robert Burns provides a satirical account
of a Communion season in Ayrshire of the 1780s:

> Here some are thinkin' on their sins,
> An' some upo' their claes;
> Ane curses feet that fyl'd his shins,
> Anither sighs an' prays:
> On this hand sits a chosen swatch,
> Wi' screw'd-up, grace-proud faces;
> On that a set of chaps, at watch,
> Thrang winkin on the lasses
> To chairs that day.

Burns's mockery is at its harshest in describing the participating
ministers and their preaching.

The sacramental occasion which brought a large number of
people, often from neighbouring parishes and too large a gathering for any country church to accommodate (as at Gairloch, p6),
usually lasted for several days, one intention being that people
could be appropriately prepared, indeed examined, before participating. The kirk session would be 'directed to the removal of

offences in the congregation and the reconciliation of people at variance'. Fast days were thought a necessary preparation for Communion. Fasts might require a day of devotion and of 'humiliation for the outbreaking of sin and wickedness in the Parish' rather than abstinence from food. Sometimes Monday was seen as a day for thanksgiving after the Sunday Communion. In many places, fast gave way to festivity - and devotion to insobriety. But well into the twentieth century, especially in the Highlands and Islands, twice-yearly Communions were usually occasions of great solemnity and spirituality, the service sometimes held out of doors, and often with a minister of note invited to preach.

It has been argued that access to Communion should be for all who have been baptized, or indeed that it should be open to all. The Church of Scotland welcomes members of all Christian churches to its Communion services. In most churches these services have been increasingly frequent, weekly in some.

The greater frequency of Communion has taken something from the sense of occasion with which Communion was once associated, especially for children. Those Easter and autumn Communions were for many children the occasion on which a church service acquired the full impact of theatre. In churches with galleries, the children were separated from, elevated above, their parents, and on this special day the children were not expected, as on other Sundays, to leave after a children's sermon in order to attend Sunday School in the church hall. Huddled together in the gallery, in varying states of reverence, they heard the solemn account of the Last Supper, they watched the elders - banker, plumber, teacher, tailor, Uncle James and Mr Thomson the lawyer - all in their dark Sunday best, some in morning coats, bring in the elements, the silver plates and cups sparkling, the tiny

The Holy Fair. Alexander Carse (1770-1843) and Robert Scott.

Hear how he clears the points o' faith
Wi' rattlin an wi' thumpin'.

(Burns)

Engᵈ by R. Scott

glasses trembling, all these distributed with careful formality to the waiting pews where the newly ironed white cloth transformed and brightened the usually bleak varnished wood. The hymns seldom varied and were sung with body and volume unique to those services, for only then was every downstairs pew filled to capacity. Upstairs children waited, nervously or naughtily, to hear how Mrs Allan or Auntie Jessie, both stalwarts in the choir, would strain and strain again, twice in every verse of Isaac Watts' 'When I Survey the Wondrous Cross' to reach the E flat, but so often failing in the attempt.

After a few years a girl or boy could become a seasoned connoisseur of the spectacle, but would soon climb no more to the gallery, being admitted then to the solemn assembly beneath.

Silver communion cups and bread plate, and a baptismal basin and ewer, seventeenth century.

Almost equal ceremony but less solemnity attended services at which baptisms took place.

Baptism of the new-born child, or of an adult, is seen by the Church of Scotland to be like Communion, a sacrament as instituted by Christ and set out in the Scriptures. Over the years Presbyterian ministers have adopted varying attitudes to baptism, some believing that infant (as opposed to adult) baptism was not appropriate; some insisting that one or both parents should be active members of the congregation and likely to fulfil promises made in the ceremony. Some have offered baptism to any child, in the church or in private. Some have denounced private baptism as papistical and have warned against any idea that there was some spiritual efficacy merely in the act of sprinkling water.

In the 1880s Andrew Edgar wrote:

> In some parishes there are ten private baptisms for every public baptism, and these private baptisms are never challenged as irregular, unlawful, or deserving of censure.

Private ceremonies often took place in the manse. One superstition decreed that a female child should never be baptized before a male child. Male supremacy, too, was maintained in the common practice that only the father (or, under certain circumstances, an approved male sponsor) took the baptismal vows. Some fathers were shy of taking vows before the whole congregation, which was one reason for baptism being performed at home.

Queen Victoria described one such christening, of the three-week-old daughter of John Thomson, a wood forester, and his wife Barbara. The minister, after an address, prayers, and a reading from Scripture, put his question to the father, who bowed assent.

> Then the minister told him -'Present your child for baptism' .
>
> After this the father took the child and held it while the minister baptised it, sprinkling it with water, but not making the sign of the cross...The service was concluded with another short prayer

and the usual blessing. I thought it most appropriate, touching and impressive. I gave my present (a silver ring) to the father, kissed the little baby, and then we all drank to its health and that of its mother in whisky, which was handed round with cakes. It was all so nicely done, so simply, and yet with such dignity.

The child was christened Victoria.

Less formal or sacramental, but common, was the custom of churching, or kirking, for which apparently the father was less necessary: mother and child simply went to church, of whatever denomination, soon after the birth. The fact of illegitimacy did not necessarily preclude baptism. In some places superstition decreed it essential that babies should be carried to church, even several miles and in any weather, at the earliest opportunity. This related in part to the common fear that the child might die before baptism or kirking. Sometimes a nurse or midwife performed a kind of baptismal ceremony to calm a mother who feared that her child was dying.

In 1931, 38,777 children were baptized in the Church of Scotland. The number rose to 50,387 in 1961: by 1993 it was 14,707.

Marriage statistics for previous centuries would, if available, tell us little that offers valid comparison. At one stage boys of fourteen and girls of twelve were free to marry. For the most part, Scots law did not hold either a religious or any other ceremony to be necessary for marriage to be established. Marriage was a consensual contract, and marriage 'by habit and repute' was legally recognized. There was a distinction between regular and irregular marriages, the former being conducted, preferably in a church, by a minister of the Church of Scotland, with banns proclaimed in the parish church prior to the wedding. Episcopalian ministers were allowed to celebrate marriages by religious ceremony from 1711, and Dissenting ministers from 1834. From the eighteenth century onwards, efforts were made to reduce the number of

Shawl worn for 'kirking', a woman's first visit to church after a wedding or christening.

clandestine or irregular marriages. The distinction between regular and irregular marriage ended in 1939 with an Act for Scotland by which marriage was religious (whether Christian or Jewish) or civil, conducted by a registrar. In 1977 a Marriage Act allowed for religious marriage in other faiths (monogamy required) and ended the proclamation of banns. By the late twentieth century Church of Scotland ministers were allowed to marry divorced persons.

The location of marriage ceremonies has varied. In 1886 Andrew Edgar wrote that marriage by Presbyterians was now seldom solemnized in church: 'the common rule in Scotland, for more than a hundred years, has been to celebrate marriage in private houses. This is done in the very teeth of the written law of the Church.' Many marriage ceremonies were conducted in the manse, probably a great deal warmer than the church. In 1993, 55 per cent of Scottish marriages were held in churches or conducted by ministers, a decline from 87 per cent in the 1930s.

There was sad acceptance by the Church of Scotland General Assembly of the fact that by the 1990s many couples approaching the altar had already cohabited. In previous times proclamation of banns was refused to, and discipline imposed upon, those who were 'under scandal'. Some courting customs, however, seem to have involved widespread acceptance of scandal. It was accepted in some communities that a man might wish to confirm in advance of marriage that a woman could have children. In the nineteenth century high figures for illegitimacy were attributed by concerned churchmen in part to housing conditions, also to working conditions on farms.

There are many records of earnest concern that on the occasion of weddings people should 'dine or cup temperately, as becometh Christians'. Attempts were made to limit the numbers attending; to forbid piping, especially by 'striking up incongruous tunes', or dancing or the 'discharging of loose speeches, singing of bawdy songs, and profane minstrelling' during the wedding feast. Such concerns persisted over the years, at times focusing on the excessive consumption of alcohol, a problem which arose especially at penny weddings. At these, as many as two or three hundred people might be gathered for two or more days, all contributing to the cost, usually by supplying food and drink, 'then the common form of marriage present'.

In the seventeenth century the 'hostlers and changers of meat and drink' in Galston secured an astonishing beneficence from the local kirk session 'anent the halding and keiping of brydall diners, burialls and baptisme diners'. Evidently 'hostlers in the landwart [had] rypit the most part of the benefits of the conventiones foresaid', to which competitive commercial practice the kirk session obligingly put an end.

Death, like marriage, brought family and community together. In many places when a member of the family was judged to be at death's door, relations and neighbours gathered in the house and united in worship, singing psalms suited to the occasion, such as the 23rd:

> Yea, though I walk in death's dark vale,
> yet will I fear none ill.

or the 118th:

> This is the gate of God, by it
> the just shall enter in.

Clearly these were devout churchfolk drawing upon religious resources they knew well. In many homes religious observance was accompanied by a liberal admixture of superstitious practice.

Reformers decreed that the disposal of the dead should take place 'without all kind of ceremony heretofore used', without either singing or reading, and without superstitious usages 'but with such gravity and sobriety as those that be present may seeme to fear the judgment of God, and to hate sin, which is the cause of death'. For the Reformers, sin embraced more than now seems appropriate, and superstition referred as much to papist practice as to ancient folklore. Churchmen argued vigorously in the nineteenth century about whether prayers should be said at funerals.

In the 1930s J R Fleming, a church historian, wrote 'Funeral services within living memory were so bleak and barren that often not a word was spoken at the grave. Now it is universal to hold them there as well as in the house of mourning, the hallowed sentences of committal to the dust giving expression to the inextinguishable hope of immortality.' Presbyterian churchmen repudiated the idea of churchyards being holy ground but they still thought the environs of the church to be appropriate for the burial of Christians. For one thing, such burial ensured that proper records were kept and proper supervision maintained of the allocation, digging and maintenance of graves.

From before the Reformation there survived in some old churches the practice of burial under the church floor. Some communities and some families of position maintained this right but, for obvious reasons, of space and sanitation, it became customary for interment to take place outside. People wished to be buried in the neighbourhood of a church, also to have their houses close to the church. The proximity of houses to churches had mixed results, for some householders threw their rubbish into the churchyard, but the houses and the high walls around the churchyard helped to keep unwanted people and animals from

Beggars' badges (sometimes called tokens, medals or tickets) made from pewter or lead, were issued, often by kirk sessions, to authorize certain paupers to beg in the parish.

the graves. The unwanted people in the early nineteenth century were grave-robbers stealing bodies to be sold to medical schools. To prevent this gruesome practice, watch-houses were built and iron cages or mortsafes were placed on graves.

Among those gathered round the deceased, at 'lykewakes', there was probably a church elder acting as the local inspector delegated to check that the shroud was made of the material (now Scots linen, now wool) required by the law of the time. It was also customary for the kirk session to be responsible for ensuring provision of bier or coffin (when the family was too poor to afford one) or the supplying, for a fee, of the appropriate style of mort-cloth to cover the coffin. For economy, a re-usable 'slip-coffin' was used by some, the body slipping out of the coffin as it was lowered in the grave. All such services provided by the kirk session involved either the exacting of a fee or the use of fee-money to help the poor. In fact the costs of provision for appropriate burial of the poor became part-cause of what is said to have been the first imposition of local rates.

Many accounts of rituals surrounding death refer to 'services': these were not religious services but were usually generous services of food and drink to the relatives and friends who gathered

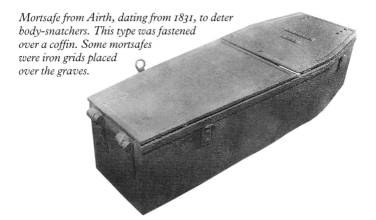

Mortsafe from Airth, dating from 1831, to deter body-snatchers. This type was fastened over a coffin. Some mortsafes were iron grids placed over the graves.

for the lykewake. Grace was usually said before each 'service', sometimes a prayer of thanksgiving afterwards, the religious element depending on the strength of church allegiance, on the availability of a minister or of an elder blessed with the 'gift' of prayer.

There were often long journeys to burials because people wished to be laid to rest in a distant family grave. The funeral procession was often more impressive than the simple ritual of interment, for people marked the occasion by lining the country roads or crowding the city streets, as when Thomas Chalmers in 1847 and Hugh Miller in 1856 were taken to their rest, in Edinburgh's Grange Cemetery. By the nineteenth century an increasing number of graveyards were some distance from churches. By the twentieth, an ever-increasing number of funeral ceremonies were held in churches or crematoria chapels, sometimes both. While church membership was falling, ministers were still being asked to conduct funerals, which may be seen as a modern preference for service by an acknowledged professional, or perhaps as a sign, or an echo, of an 'inextinguishable hope'.

In many parts of Scotland both before and after the Reformation people celebrated saints' days and holy days, welcoming them as holidays. Some Reformers saw observances of the Christian year as papist inventions, the Lord's Day alone having Scriptural authority. We find days associated with St Serf, St Cowie, St Couslan, St Barr, St Peter, St Flannan, St Bride and others marked in district calendars as holidays and occasions for festivity. In the nineteenth century fast-day holidays were increasingly frowned upon by some employers in industrial areas. By the late twentieth century in urban areas the long-established and colourful annual harvest thanksgiving had lost much of its meaning or impact, for supermarkets offered the same fruits all the year round, and many city children had no experience or knowledge of the fruitfulness of autumn.

Hogmanay and New Year's Day have for long been days for festivity in Scotland. From Isabella Morrice's account of childhood in the 1890s, within a fervently religious family circle in Aberdeen, we find that Santa Claus arrived a week after Christmas:

> It was on Hogmanay night that we hung up our stockings and on New Year's Day our aunts called with books for us and we read them in grandeur beside the parlour fire. We always got an orange, an apple, a slice of cake and a Santa Claus stocking and not much if anything else, perhaps a copper or two and a few sweets. On 30 December we went to the carriers to get a parcel from Uncle Tom, the most generous of our relations. On one of the days of that week we also collected a parcel from Auntie Montgarrie from the Alford carrier. It was a carpet bag and there was a hen for each household. The carpet bag went back full of comforts.

Christmas Day was very much a working day in urban areas. However, in some places Christmas, indeed Christmas week, had been noted for festivities (not worship) especially among the better-off, though lesser mortals were glad to join in:

> Yule's come and Yule's gane
> And we hae feasted weel;
> Sae Jock maun to his flail again
> And Jenny to her wheel.

(Fife rhyme)

In general Christmas was increasingly recognized, but in moderation and not so much as Hogmanay and New Year's Day. In the 1950s many Scots were still at work on Christmas Day but very few on New Year's Day.

In churches where hymns were being sung in the late nineteenth century the Christmas hymns, most of them written in the previous 100 years, were becoming familiar, and many carols dating back to the fifteenth century were being revived. In the early twentieth century Sunday Schools began having Christmas parties and city churches had Christmas services to which children brought gifts for the poor. The Sunday School child in

Scottish Presbyterian communities of the 1930s had probably never heard of Advent, or of Lent. After the Second World War the next generation became familiar with Advent calendars as part of a highly commercialized period leading up to Christmas.

Some Presbyterian churchmen began to show interest in the Christian year in the late nineteenth century. By 1940 the Church of Scotland was accepting a Book of Common Order which noted the calendar of the Christian Year but included only one Saint's Day, that of St Andrew, patron saint of Scotland. Easter had for long been observed as the occasion for one of the two main Communion gatherings, or Sacramental Occasions, of the year - as noted above. Although Communion services became more frequent throughout the year, Easter lost little of its importance, services being held in some churches throughout Holy Week as well.

10 Change or decline

In its report to the Church of Scotland General Assembly in 1995 the Church's Board of Parish Education argued that since the 1950s, peak years of numerical strength in church membership and Sunday School numbers, there had been 'a cultural sea-change' affecting many aspects of society: all institutions then at their zenith had declined. The Church, the report said, should 'recognize and respond to the needs of a society now living in post-institutional, post-membership culture'.

Over the centuries the Christian Church has responded to a number of sea-changes. A report in the Dark Ages would presumably have recorded the movement of Christianity into the monasteries, and in medieval times Christianity's move into the parish churches would surely have been noted. The Reformation resulted in part from the arrival of printing and the growth of literacy. The Roman Church fiercely resisted the early printing and wide distribution of the Bible in the vernacular. The Reformation, however, engaged people in Bible-centred, institutional

1950s service at Craigiebuckler Church, Aberdeen.

churches which aimed to ensure knowledge and understanding of Scripture.

For more than 200 years, until literacy was widespread, much of what was written in Scotland was by ministers, and for comparatively few readers, many of them ministers. The printed word provided a large measure of support for the Presbyterian church, mirroring it and often helping to mould it - eventually to remould it, as happened when the Scottish Enlightenment offered both challenge to and diversion from church dominance. One church leader prominent in the Enlightenment was William Robertson (1721-93), historian and academic. He was eventually seen as a leader of Moderate churchmen, as opposed to Evangelicals, in the conflict - religious, ecclesiastical, political and social - which would by mid-nineteenth century disrupt the Church of Scotland.

The growing literacy of the nineteenth century helped more and more people to respond to and contribute to the changes taking place in church and society. Among the many writers who played a part in the thinking and rethinking of the time were the two Evangelical leaders, cleric and lay respectively, Thomas Chalmers (1780-1847) and Hugh Miller (1802-56). Chalmers' numerous published works show a man alight with passion to help the poor and to enrich the role of the church in the community. Miller - stonemason, geologist, bank accountant, poet, journalist - wrote passionately on the then sensitive topic of the relationship between church and state. He fiercely attacked patronage in the appointment of ministers. His writings on a wide range of subjects, not least geology, were to achieve great popularity.

Religion featured prominently in books published in Scotland in the nineteenth century. In the world of Scottish fiction, from Scott up to the early twentieth century, churches and churchmen may often have been shown to have great faults. They appeared nevertheless as figures of undeniable consequence in their communities. With the coming, in mid to late nineteenth century, of cheaper newspapers, periodicals and books - and the further spread of literacy - churchgoers were made increasingly aware of vigorous challenge to long-accepted church attitudes, also of the growing availability of reading material which was little concerned with church affairs. At the same time the growth of literacy contributed to a kind of publication, book or periodical, that was strongly supportive to the churchgoing world. There were the worthy books given as school and Sunday School prizes and then retained as profitable family reading. Such books were recommended by the Onward and Upward Association (founded in 1891 by Lady Aberdeen 'for the material, mental and moral elevation of women'). Many of these worthy books were the products of the Religious Tract Society, for example *Sunday School Romances* by Alfred B Cooper, *Odd* by Amy le Feuvre ('a graceful and touching story, full of gospel teaching), *The Seven Wise Men* by S R Crockett. All of these were reviewed favourably by such journals as *The Sunday School Chronicle, The School Guardian, The Christian World* and probably also by *The British Weekly*, a publication edited by a remarkable Scottish minister, the Rev William Robertson Nicoll (1851-1923), son of the Rev Harry Nicoll (above).

A journalist of immense influence in politics as in church affairs, Nicoll was knighted and made a Companion of Honour. As editor of *The British Weekly* he commissioned articles by renowned churchmen and a remarkable range of literary men. *The British Weekly* was read by churchgoers of several denominations and provided for ministers, church members and others, convenient access to broadly liberal thinking in politics, religion, literature and life in general. Nicoll 'made popular journalism literary and he made religious journalism interesting'. In his journals and through the publishing house of Hodder and Stoughton he promoted the writing of such authors as Annie S Swan, J M Barrie, Samuel Rutherford Crockett and Ian Maclaren (John Watson). This group, especially the three men, have been given the dismissive title of 'Kailyard'. They deserve mention here because so much that they wrote was church-centred, and they were read with enthusiasm by many church folk, people who were coming to novels for the first time. But many of these people were also reading, for instance in *The British Weekly*, markedly serious and often demanding material on religion, literature and politics.

For all of Nicoll's authors, and for their readers, Scotland was a place in which the Bible, its stories and its language were common currency. At the end of the twentieth century, however, churches are no longer seen by Scotland's writers as central to Scottish social life, nor has the Bible been a prominent part of their upbringing. Scottish writing, like Scottish art, neither assumes nor reveals wide interest in or knowledge of religion and the church. The change has been rapid since the 1930s and 40s, a time when, for instance, the popular Glasgow poet W D Cocker, most of whose poems first appeared in the Glasgow-based newspapers, *Daily Record* and *Evening News*, was able to assume Bible knowledge in the readership of these publications. Adam and Eve, Elisha, Joseph, Pharoah, Moses, Naaman, Ruth, Balaam, Abraham, Cain and Abel, Daniel - Cocker retold all their stories in comic verse. In contrast, the *Daily Record* in December 1995 ran a £50,000 'Christmas Advent Scratchcard' competition which required no biblical knowledge on the part of contestants, and betrayed a marked indifference to religious sensitivities. Such indifference would have been unthinkable in a Glasgow newspaper of the 1950s.

The sea-change after mid-century to which the 1995 Church of Scotland report refers involved a general relaxing of attitudes by churches themselves to all entertainments, as to developments in sport and travel. The family car became the norm. Mobility in employment, as part of work and in career advancement, has dislodged family groupings and religious affiliations. Throughout the century the stability of Christian faith has been substantially disturbed in many ways - by advances, for instance, in science and medicine. Equally threatening have been challenges from society, from man's inhumanity to man, from loss of traditional respect by youth for age, from those who have found the churches themselves at fault in their apparent identification at times with war or racism or social injustice. And within the churches there have been unsettling conflicts on concepts of reverence, on the role of women, on sexual orientation, on charismatic evangelism and cults, and on Christian attitudes to other religions. The media have given prominence to all of these issues. No medium, however, no agent of change, has had greater impact in the twentieth century than broadcasting which, ironically, was seen by at least one famous Scot as capable of buttressing the Church and church attendance.

The first BBC station in Scotland was opened in 1923. The head of the BBC was John Reith, son of a Free Church minister. Searching for a BBC regional director in Scotland in 1933 he found the Rev Melville Dinwiddie, then minister of St Machar's

The old Free Church manse at Cantray, Croy, near Inverness, built in the 1850s and now in ordinary residential

Cathedral in Aberdeen. Dinwiddie held the position of Scottish BBC Controller until 1957. He eventually wrote a book *Religion by Radio* which carried a Foreword by Reith in which Reith declared 'religion by radio' to have been ineffectual, not because of failure or inadequacy in what was broadcast but because of the churches' failure to follow up and capitalize on what was so freely and generously promoted in religious broadcasts. If only, he said, the churches had moved in to encourage those whose interest had been revived by broadcast religion, 'there might have been a national revival on a scale hitherto unimagined'.

When Reith wrote this, religious broadcasting and the hours usually associated with church services were afforded some degree of protection, and religion on radio and television in BBC Scotland was still under the direction of the Rev Ronald Falconer who from 1945 to 1971 ensured a remarkable provision from Scotland of broadcast church services, of General Assembly coverage, religious documentaries, discussion and talks. In the early 1960s BBC Scotland was providing nearly half of all BBC religious television on Scottish screens, a sizeable proportion, too, of all that BBC Scotland itself was providing. Under Falconer's aegis, several Scottish churchmen became TV personalities in Scotland. Evangelical campaigns were given prominent coverage, including Kirk Weeks and the Tell Scotland movement, which lasted for much of a decade and at one point featured Billy Graham, the American evangelist. Probably the most impressive impact of all was made by the series of radio and television lectures, and also sermons, by the Rev Professor William Barclay. In gruff and rough Scots tones, speaking with directness and simplicity, he captivated viewers, though he also enraged many jealous divines. His broadcasts helped promote his numerous books. The New Testament volumes of his Daily Study Bible series, published in a number of languages, sold six million copies and over some years ensured the financial security of the Church

Professor William Barclay rehearsing for a television broadcast.

of Scotland's St Andrew Press. The sales figures indicate that it was not only church ministers who bought Barclay's books.

Listening to Barclay was like listening to resounding teaching-preaching in a great Scottish tradition. Other ministers, on BBC and independent television, have sometimes been impressive too, though it is noteworthy that some men with great reputations as popular preachers failed to make much impression on television, no matter the setting or the support. The BBC in Scotland was, in fact, engaged in a most remarkable rearguard action involving the church, the printed word and both radio and television. But by the time Falconer retired, his message was clearly too much for the medium. Fewer BBC services of worship were broadcast from Scotland though many more hours of television were broadcast. It was argued by the broadcasters that they should address the changing situation in which church attendance was decreasing, and that 'spiritual understanding' should be promoted in a variety of, often experimental, programme formats.

Some television drama, like ITV's 'Jesus of Nazareth' has tackled biblical themes, with varying success. The most noteworthy survivor of BBC religious television programmes has been the Sunday evening 'Songs of Praise' which has come from all parts of the UK and from abroad. It normally includes several hymns, a few interviews and a short prayer, but no teaching-preaching sermons; these, along with services of a traditional kind, are mostly relegated to radio. ITV, on the other hand, has continued to offer Scottish viewers some traditional services on Sunday mornings. Hogmanay in 1995 was on a Sunday and Scottish viewers preparing for New Year were able to watch the first-ever 'Songs of Praise on Ice' which came from Blackpool Pleasure Beach. The vigorous singing, often to lively syncopated music, was accompanied by ice dancing, some of it choreographed enactments of the Christmas story.

In 1996 neither the BBC nor independent television chose to broadcast a Billy Graham 'televangelist' programme available by cable and satellite to an estimated 2.5 billion world audience.

Cable and satellite may find audiences for the evangelical 'Stay Tuned, Stay Blessed' approach, which has had some ratings success in North America. But it is uncertain whether, at the end of the twentieth century, many churchmen of any faith in Scotland see broadcast religion as an acceptable alternative, rather than at best an occasional stimulant, to churchgoing. Broadcast worship may allow two or three million in the UK to be gathered 'in His name' but not as a definable group providing support to an institutional church. The medium of broadcasting has, in fact, contributed to no 'national revival', to use Reith's phrase. The same goes for the medium of print, also for cinema and theatre. To none of these, from mid-century onwards, could the churches look for support in relation either to religious belief or to what had been conventional morality. As for religious education in schools, the Board of Education report accepted that non-Catholic churches were 'no longer in the driving seat'. The Church of Scotland may still be described as the established church in Scotland, but the concept has become something of a dated formality.

In Scotland over the centuries, the churches have played an appreciable and mostly creditable role in the politics, education and social life of the nation. In future they may be in turn the agents and the victims of change, but there is no apparent inclination to turn the clock back. Churchgoers are not likely to wish for a return to the pervasive church dominance of the eighteenth century, to the painfully long sermons, the monotony and often discord of the music, the punitive fatalism that permeated much of the theology, the exclusiveness of access to Communion, the varied forms and effects of patronage (the duties and rights of heritors ended in the 1920s).

Many of the attitudes and changes of the nineteenth century have been traced in these pages. The diversity which developed in the nineteenth century had much to recommend it, but there was also bitterness and a great waste of resources in the divisions among Protestant churches and between Protestants and Catholics. As

Catholics increased in numbers, religious and social animosity grew. Fortunately, the most striking and the most reassuring contrast in any comparison between the Scottish churches at the beginning and at the end of the twentieth century lies in the easing of tensions between all of the denominations, not least between Protestants and Catholics. Action of Churches Together in Scotland (ACTS) was founded in 1990. The Roman Catholic Church is a full member along with eight other denominations.

No Scottish churchman may be more clearly identified with the new ecumenism of the twentieth century than the Very Rev Dr A C Craig (1888-1985). He became General Secretary to the British Council of Churches and as Church of Scotland Moderator (1961-2) made official visits to Pope John XXIII (the first ever such meeting) and to the three Patriarchs of Jerusalem, Orthodox, Latin and Armenian. Dr Craig delighted in telling of an old Scotswoman who, after hearing him read the prologue to St John's Gospel, said to him 'Was it no a wunnerfu thing that the Son o God cam doon in that mainner that a puir ill-learnit auld body like me could "grup" him !' In one broadcast interview, however, when asked by Ronald Falconer if he himself had had personal religious experiences, Dr Craig said 'Yes I have but I am not going to tell you about them. There is such a thing as spiritual indecency.'

This reaction of paradoxical reserve, from one of the most eloquently articulate of churchmen, highlights the inescapable difficulty in any attempt to estimate what people gain from their religion or from going to church. We may describe the prayer, the song, the sermon, the silence, the ambience, the community - a remarkable package indeed - but the experience itself, for individual or community, does not readily submit to definition. Some people make the attempt, with varying degrees of success. For many, the word and song provided in church worship serve as appropriate, if still less than adequate, expression. The practice is long-established of using other people's words to express emotion and conviction, indeed to validate experience.

In one sermon, on Christianity and Catastrophe, Dr Craig presented the image of the Bible as 'the campfire at which western man has sought reassurance in face of the darkness and dangers of our mortal journey'. For the benefit of churchgoers, he said, preachers poke industriously at the Bible, valiantly blowing at their texts 'out of our own little lungs'. Preachers may have to blow especially hard now that the texts, variously worded in so many different translations, are inevitably less familiar to the churchgoer. Many well-known hymns, too, are being edited out of hymnbooks and losing their place in worship. Various translations of the Psalms are on offer, but the metrical Psalms, now hallowed by more than three centuries of use in Scotland, have proved peculiarly resistant to change. The metrical Psalm with which most Scots people must now be most familiar is 'The Lord's My Shepherd' (Psalm 23) which is almost invariably sung at funerals, still so well attended. This Psalm, replete with personal reassurance, ends:

> And in God's house for evermore
> My dwelling place shall be.

Those who know their Bibles well - in any translation, prose or metrical - will know that they need not go to church to be 'in God's house', which may be a reassuring thought for the non-churchgoer. In today's 'post-institutional, post-membership culture', however, preachers may prefer to blow valiantly at another Old Testament text ('Nec Tamen Consumebatur' Exodus 3.2) which is to be found on the crest which has been used for more than three centuries by the Church of Scotland. The crest shows the Burning Bush:

> And the Angel of the Lord appeared unto Moses in a flame of fire out of the midst of a bush; and he looked, and, behold, the bush burned with fire, and the bush was not consumed.

FURTHER READING

BURLEIGH, J H S *A Church History of Scotland*, Oxford 1960

CAMERON, Nigel M de S ed *Dictionary of Scottish Church History and Theology*, Edinburgh 1993

DONALDSON, Gordon *The Faith of the Scots*, London 1990

DRUMMOND, Andrew L and BULLOCH, James *The Church in Victorian Scotland 1843-1874*, Edinburgh 1975

HENDERSON, G D *The Church of Scotland*, Edinburgh 1939

LINDSAY, Ian G *The Scottish Parish Kirk*, Edinburgh 1960

MACLEAN, Allan *Telford's Highland Churches*, Coll 1989

PATRICK, Millar *Four Centuries of Scottish Psalmody*, Oxford 1949

TULLOCH, Graham *A History of the Scots Bible*, Aberdeen 1989

PLACES TO VISIT

There are more than 4,000 places of worship in Scotland. At least 60 substantially medieval churches are still in use, probably the oldest and least altered of these being St Cuthbert's Parish Kirk, Dalmeny. The following museums and historic sites display material related to the history of Christianity in Scotland:

Aberdeen: St Andrews Cathedral
Arbroath: Arbroath Abbey; St Vigeans
Biggar: Greenhill Covenanters' House
Blantyre: David Livingstone Centre
Dunblane: Dunblane Cathedral Museum
Dunkeld: Dunkeld Cathedral Chapter House Museum
Edinburgh: John Knox House
Glasgow: St Mungo Museum
Iona: Iona Abbey Museum
Melrose: Melrose Abbey
Mintlaw: Deer Abbey
St Andrews: St Andrews Cathedral
Stranraer: Castle of St John
Whithorn: Whithorn Priory

The new Museum of Scotland, due to open in late 1998, will include displays on early Christianity, the Medieval Church, the Reformed Church and Christian worship in the eighteenth and nineteenth centuries.